How To Start and Run

# A
# ONE
# PERSON
# BUSINESS

# How To Start and Run

# A
# ONE
# PERSON
# BUSINESS

## CLIVE MORTON

**howto**books

Constable & Robinson Ltd
55—56 Russell Square
London WC1B 4HP
www.constablerobinson.com

First published in the UK by How To Books,
an imprint of Constable & Robinson Ltd, 2013

A copy of the British Library Cataloguing in
Publication Data is available from the British Library

ISBN 978-1-84528-503-6

Typeset by TW Typesetting, Plymouth, Devon

Printed and bound in the UK

1 3 5 7 9 10 8 6 4 2

# Contents

**Preface**                                                                    ix

**1   Starting a service-based business**                                       1

Understanding the common ground in all one
    person businesses                                       2

Professional services                                                          3

Management services                                                            3

Personal services                                                              3

Product-based services                                                         4

**2   The advantages of self-employment**                                       5

Using your skills to provide a personal service                                5

Planning your business to mitigate risk                                        6

Charging for your services                                                     7

Considering other benefits of self-employment                                  9

**3   Understanding yourself and your aspirations**                            10

Dealing with the public                                                        10

Selling your service or product                                                11

Setting realistic goals                                                        12

Believing in yourself                                                          12

Thinking about numbers                                                         13

**4   Defining your market**                                                   14

Services to the public                                                         14

Think hard about where the business is coming
    from before you commit                                  16

Specialist businesses and internet 24
The nature of the buying decision 29

**5 Studying competition** **33**
Services to the public 33
Pricing 34
Time and how you use it 35
Keeping an eye on competitors 35
Services to industry 36
Study how the product or service is sold 36

**6 Specifying your product or service** **40**
Analysis of the factors 40
Setting objectives 42
Skilled trades 43
Personal services 45
Professional services 46
Services to commercial undertakings 47
Agency, general trading, internet and mail order 50

**7 A different approach for creative ideas** **52**
Bringing creative ideas to market 55

**8 Marketing** **59**
Skilled trades 59
Personal services 63
Professional services 65
Services to industry 66
Sales agents 71
General trading, internet and mail order 75

Creative people 77

Inventors 82

**9 Pricing your product or service 86**

Skilled trades 87

Personal services 91

Professional services 92

Management services 94

General trading, internet and mail order 97

Agents 100

Creative people 101

**10 Calculating risk and breakeven 105**

What to do if you do not get an order for six

months 106

Trade services to the public 107

Personal services 109

Professional services 110

Management services to industry 112

Internet trading, mail order, etc. 113

Agents 117

Creative occupations 117

**11 Using other services and professionals 119**

Tradesmen 121

Personal services 124

Professional services 126

Management services 126

Selling via the internet, mail order, etc. 127

Sales agents 129

Creative people                                         129
Dealing with banks                                      130

**12   A basic understanding of commercial law          139**
Contract law                                            141
Sale of goods                                           144

**13   Tax implications and structuring                 146**
Record keeping                                          148
Operating through a limited company                     151
Value added tax (VAT)                                   152

**14   Employing staff                                  154**
Your own role in the business                           155
The job description                                     156
Job advertisement                                       157
The job interview                                       159
Contract of employment                                  161
Affirmation of the contract                             162

**15   Acquiring or renting property                    163**
A lease                                                 164
Sub-tenancies                                           166
Licences                                                167
Other                                                   167

**16   Expansion problems                               169**
Know yourself                                           170

**Index                                                 173**

# *Preface*

## Several million people have already struck out on their own – why don't you join them?

Napoleon once said, 'England is a nation of shopkeepers'. It was intended as a derogatory remark but, in fact, pointed to the independent streak in many of our countrymen who, even 200 years ago, supported themselves and built a lifestyle from their own efforts – a heritage of which we should all feel proud.

Certainly running your own business is not for the work shy. In the early years you probably work longer hours than most of your former workmates and you have to handle administrative functions at the end of the day, such as raising invoices, keeping records and planning the next job. But for most of us who do our own thing, there is greater job satisfaction, a sense of achievement and, once established, greater financial rewards. I have run my own businesses for more than 30 years and cannot envisage a job offer that would tempt me to work for somebody else. I have had my share of ups and downs but now, in later life, I have a sense of freedom and independence that is not available to most employees.

In my earlier career I ran other people's businesses in the packaging, engineering and toy industries before launching out, practising as an accountant and business consultant providing services to smaller companies. Many of my friends operate their own companies and I enjoy analysing the formulae, prospects and limitations of various business concepts. It is my view that business pays for everything and is badly treated in the UK, an over-governed society run by bureaucrats who do not have the balls to run a company but enjoy telling everybody else what to do. Without businesses we would quickly revert to almost pre-historic conditions. Business gives employment to the masses in every country. Employees and businesses pay the taxes that fund the government who use the taxes to employ more people, most of whom lack the nous to understand that their incomes are derived from business, not from some political party handing out largess in order to win votes.

Today, as I write, the country is in dire straits, largely due to being mismanaged by people who lack business experience and do not understand the nature of competition or the constant need for innovation, and product and efficiency improvements.

For most of my life the UK has been in the top five largest economies in the world. If we are to remain even among the top ten, it will be done by creating new businesses that ultimately give gainful employment to committed workers, pay reasonable taxes and contribute to a growing national output. This will not be brought about by politicians and public servants, although they could help by cutting red tape and interfering less often.

So if you are thinking of starting a new business be assured that it is one of the most important contributions a person can make to their country.

Your own rewards will be personal growth, greater independence and financial benefits.

So read on to learn how to accomplish these ends and, when you do launch out, keep this manual handy for future reference.

# 1 *Starting a service-based business*

For those of you who lack funds to invest but who, nevertheless, want to own and run a business of your own, the opportunities are more restricted than for those with a reasonable lump sum available and the assets to back borrowings. Almost any business, however, requires some investment. This is usually in the form of income sacrifice for a period of time until the business is up and running, or you may have to allocate part of your home to the business for use as an office, studio or consulting room, etc.

The business opportunities are likely to be restricted to those that offer a service rather than a product, as products cost money to stock and deliver.

For those of you who lack the funds to invest it is most likely that you will offer a service, based on your personal skills, although it may be possible to act as a sales agent and sell other people's products or to trade on the internet. At this stage, however, we will talk about services. Those available may be classified into groups under the following headings:

- Provision of services to the general public

- Provision of services to commercial undertakings and/ or government

- Creative concepts – authors, artists, inventors, etc.

## Understanding the common ground in all one person businesses

I want to stress a fundamental point at this stage that in all one person businesses you will be providing a service or a product to either the general public or to commercial businesses/government departments and, in some cases, to both. In everything I have written, and will be further writing about, I am looking at the common ground these services and products share. I fully understand that an architect's training and background and the nature of their work is entirely different from that of a beauty therapist or plasterer. In creating a business, however, they face many similar problems.

It is for the individual to understand the nature of their own skills and the special features of their trades or professions; the management techniques I describe apply to, and can be used in every business, and so I ask all my readers to think about what I say in relation to their chosen occupation and to bear in mind that, if they want to succeed, they will also need to acquire some general management skills, depending on how far they want to grow their businesses. I shall also deal with practical application of commercial law in relation to running a business.

## Professional services

Professional services usually, but not always, require the clients to visit the professional. This is partly traditional and partly associated with costs because it is widely understood and accepted that professional services are charged by the hour and, therefore, travel to the client would add to the final bill. There are, of course, many exceptions to this, such as where architects and surveyors need to visit premises and sites, but much of their work is still carried out in offices.

## Management services

Management services form a growing category as many middle-aged managers, in particular, have a range of skills and experience but find themselves frustrated or redundant and/or in a situation where they cannot increase their incomes, and often have to accept lower remuneration. For such people self-employment could and should be the perfect antidote so this, too, will be treated as a further separate group.

## Personal services

Personal services embrace a wide range of skills that probably, in the early stages, necessitate visiting clients, although with most it is preferable to have clients visit you, once adequate premises are affordable.

## Product-based businesses

For those of you who want to deal in products, albeit with limited means, I will also be discussing agency and internet selling as a separate issue in each chapter, where appropriate. Indeed, all the above categories will be dealt with separately, where different approaches apply, but a substantial part of each section will apply to all groups.

In each chapter I will be outlining the subject under discussion under the above categories headings. This will enable you to focus on your chosen occupation and skip the sections that do not currently apply to you. Businesses do grow and change, however, so I urge you to retain this book as a work of reference. Much of what I say is common sense and many of you will instinctively follow the practices outlined, although many will not automatically consider the pre-planning activities I advocate. The manner in which you set yourself up is critical to your success and this is why I have dedicated the first few chapters to these considerations.

# 2 The advantages of self-employment

The internet today is awash with advertisements and PR describing how, by buying simple systems, you can make so much money trading currencies, commodities, stocks and shares in half an hour a day, or by using a betting system, that you could quit work and sit on the beach. I doubt there is a single system that has achieved even a small profit for anyone, let alone a fortune. Some people are genuinely lucky and somebody does win the lottery most weeks but, for most of us, the only way to a fortune is through hard work, objectivity and enterprise.

## Using your skills to provide a personal service

In this book I am writing for people who want to use their skills to provide a personal service from whatever walk of life or simply trade products. This is essentially about businesses that can be started and run from your home with little or no capital investment. The primary distinction in this edition is entry into a business occupation where you do most, if not all, of the work. I am writing here for the individual who has ability but limited funds and so wants a low risk start that can be achieved with limited financial resources.

## Planning your business to mitigate risk

Even so, starting a one person business is not without risk and needs planning with care and, if possible, making contact with people who could be helpful before giving up your job. If, however, circumstances are such that you are already out of work, for whatever reason, the matter assumes greater urgency.

The problems of starting a one person business have several factors in common, regardless of former occupations and background skills. People from all walks of life have become self-employed – artists, salesmen, carpenters, nurses, teachers and managers from within all types of companies and particularly within the professions, most of which have a long tradition of giving independent advice to clients. Many of these turn into partnerships or limited companies. These issues will be discussed in later chapters.

People within the medical profession have a particular problem in that they are likely to be competing with a free National Health Service but, even here, practitioners have managed to set up as private doctors, physiotherapists, health counsellors and many other specialist services.

# Charging for your services

An initial calculation is needed that is largely about money, but other factors need consideration such as where is the business going to come from, but one thing is reasonably sure that **if you can capture sufficient business to occupy your time, your income should more than double, compared to the income achieved in employment**.

The reason is simple. Professional firms, in particular, typically charge out employees at three times what they pay them, i.e. if you are employed at £40,000 p.a. the cost to your employer is circa £45,000 for probably 45 weeks of work, net of holidays and illness, or £1,000 per week. You are almost certainly being charged out at £3,000 per week or £600 per day. It may be that while you build your practice up you can only charge £400 per day but this is double your former income.

Tradesmen are not charged by their employers at quite as high a rate as professionals, but £50/60 per hour is typical outside London, or £300/375 per day at an effective 75 per cent saleability of time. Plumbers, electricians and plasterers are probably paid more than a third of this rate because of a scarcity factor. This indicates that an annual income approaching six figures is available to the self-employed tradesman.

The arithmetic is not quite so clear in other occupations but a salesman could quickly judge the volume required to double their income if they became a commission agent. The nature of the product being sold has a more significant bearing on income levels in these cases than occupational skills, i.e. computer and highly technical salesmen would expect to earn more than door-to-door salesmen. Sales negotiators in estate agents' businesses could reap much higher returns but there is probably an up-front capital or investment cost in such cases.

Many of the managerial opportunities for self-employment would necessitate capital investment – setting up advertising agencies, buying franchises or running small businesses – but considerable scope exists in what could loosely be described as the consultancy market. HR managers can move into training, job evaluation and employment policy areas as a consultant and secure high fees. IT can bring high rewards although keeping up to date can prove onerous in the longer term. For senior managers a rich seam is opening up in coaching other senior executives. Much of this work is of a very personal nature.

Hair stylists, beauty therapists, masseurs, physiotherapists and so on probably ultimately need salons, but many such businesses have been successfully launched by visiting clients at home initially or by becoming part of a multi-service facility where rentals are shared to help keep costs down.

## Considering other benefits of self-employment

Much of the foregoing is about money and rightly so. It has to be worthwhile to take risk and commit to long hours in the early stages. Other benefits arise once established: **freedom from interference by bosses and a sense of independence, constantly meeting new people, improved lifestyle, greater self-awareness, a sense of achievement and respect within the community.** If set up correctly there are certain tax advantages, and these are dealt with in a later chapter.

# 3 *Understanding yourself and your aspirations*

As described in the previous chapter, people from almost any walk of life can establish and build a one person business. It is equally true that most types of person are able to do so. You do not have to be exceptionally intelligent – indeed this is sometimes a disadvantage and many intellectuals see too many problems that ultimately inhibit them from taking any action. You do, however, need to be competent at what you do, i.e. if you plan to provide office cleaning services it is essential you leave the offices clean. Sounds obvious, but equally if you plan to set up as a solicitor you cannot afford to be wrong on points of law. Businesses are built on reputation, a subject we will discuss later.

## Dealing with the public

There are certain common threads in running a solo enterprise of almost any nature, the most important of which is **people**. Life is lived among people and if your business is in any way related to serving the general public or certain sectors you are going to be dealing with people constantly. They are your customers and it is bad business to upset them or quarrel with them. It is often said the customer is always right. This isn't true, but there is, nevertheless, a way of convincing them otherwise without coming to blows. It follows, therefore, that if your business relies on face-to-face contact that it is desirable to have an awareness of human nature and to have reasonable communication skills. It helps if you like people.

Many occupations involve far less direct communication. Authors and artists can work in isolation but, at the end of the day, their work still has to appeal to people. In other businesses you can sell through the internet or by advertising and mail order but, in most one person businesses, sooner or later, you have to get out there among the people, your potential customers, and promote yourself and your service.

## Selling your service or product

Selling the product or service is an important part of building a successful business. In most one person operations, however, you are usually providing an expertise that your potential customers lack. They are essentially consulting you and are likely to have respect for your opinion, unless you convince them otherwise. It follows that an important aspect of the process is to listen carefully to what the customer tells you. The next part is to provide a solution to their problem. Most solo businesses are started by competent people who are viewed as experts in their fields. Customers and clients usually consult them to solve a problem.

You go to a doctor if you are sick, see a solicitor if you are charged with an offence, talk to an accountant about tax problems, call in a plumber if your central heating doesn't work and so on. In virtually all of these cases you are solving a customer's problem. If you listen, put the customer at ease and find a solution, your reputation will grow by word of mouth.

## Setting realistic goals

There is inevitably risk in taking the plunge and setting up a business but this does not mean gambling or being reckless, rather it is a calculated risk. Many successful business people err on the side of caution. Most achievements are first conceived in the mind. This does not require genius, rather objectivity. The art is to set rational goals, think how to attain them then go for them single-mindedly. **Positive thinking is a must and this implies taking responsibility.** Consider the problems that might occur and how you might deal with them so that you are ready to react when confronted. If you deal positively with them you will usually gain respect and support and often turn a bad situation to your advantage by responding in a helpful manner.

## Believing in yourself

Allied to this is determination and mental toughness. Having committed yourself to starting a business you must follow through and you must believe in yourself and in your ability to overcome obstacles. You need to set out to be an achiever; don't give in. Successful people develop an aura and are easily recognised; strive to become one and remember that problems are also opportunities. The more problems you solve the stronger you become.

## Thinking about numbers

Business is also about **numbers**. You do need basic arithmetic, although in many cases spouses and partners can and do lend support. Prices have to be set and costs identified and budgeted. Some paperwork is inevitable but this should be kept as simple as possible. Many one person businesses do <u>not</u> need computerised accounting systems; many are better off with just a file of invoices issued and another of invoices received and perhaps a summary of each. More of this later but it has to be recognised that some administration is essential and that numbers are a consideration in most aspects of business, especially when the business starts to grow.

Essentially, most people have the ability to become self-employed and be reasonably successful, at least to a level ahead of what they would have achieved in somebody else's employment. You do, however, need reasonable numeracy, communication ability, positive thinking and determination – attributes that can actually be learned or developed. They are not inborn talents. The door is wide open for most reasonably competent people.

# 4 *Defining your market*

## Services to the public

### Skilled Trades

Most one person service businesses tend to be local,
where customers can be reached or they can reach you
in comfortably under one hour. If not, too much time
is wasted travelling and customers are not keen to pay
for time spent travelling. It is therefore relatively easy to
quantify the market in your catchment area in whatever
terms you deem appropriate, i.e. number of homes,
number of children, number of cars, etc.

Information is readily available on the internet,
particularly on demographics, so that you can quickly
identify these numbers and obtain breakdowns by
a variety of categories. This will give you a quick
overview of the potential, i.e. the UK population is
slightly more than 60 million who live in approximately
24,000,000 homes or one home for 2.5 people on
average. If, for instance, your catchment area is
roughly equal to a parliamentary constituency of

circa 100,000 people or 40,000 homes, each of which requires a plumber once every four years then the market for plumbers can be assessed as 10,000 visits per year or 200 visits per week of typically four hours' duration. You can quickly estimate that the area needs approximately 20/22 plumbers. If you ascertain it already has 25 then competition is likely to be tough and you might be well advised to seek a different area. If on the other hand the area is serviced by only 18 plumbers, an opportunity exists to break into the market immediately and to charge the full going rate. (The figures are estimates but, as experts from whatever field, you can substitute more accurate numbers of visits made and their duration to assess your own market potential.)

It can be harder to quantify the market in this way in London or other major cities where there is bound to be overlap between districts, as defined by Thompson Directories or *Yellow Pages*, but some attempt should be made.

It really is vital to try to establish whether there really is a market for your service in your area, because it is a humiliating experience to put your heart and soul into setting up a business only to fail because the market is too competitive.

New building activity is a feature of the market for tradesmen, as most builders employ only a core staff and sub-contract most of the trades – roofing, electrics, plumbing and heating, plastering, joinery, etc. Sub-contracting is carried out extensively by both national and local builders so making contact with all of them could be of paramount importance. A plumber could easily spend a week in each new house installing boilers and heating systems, bathrooms and kitchen sinks, washing machines, etc. Likewise a carpenter could spend a few days fitting built-in cupboards and wardrobes.

In such cases it would also pay to plan a short presentation, stating what you have done and where you have worked and details of any particular skills you have and leave the builder with a short resumé and full contact details. Success with these types of contacts could set you up with enough work to keep you going for a year.

## Think hard about where the business is coming from before you commit

Your opportunity should be defined in market terms and in relation to your own gut feel about what you want to do. For instance, a kitchen fitter could decide they want to work on large building sites where there is continuity of work and that they might earn £30 an hour, but with scope for considerable overtime in summer months. Alternatively, they might consider that if they advertise locally as both a supplier and an installer they could charge £40 an hour and make a handling charge on the product, but without the guarantee of continued work. A further option would be to work for three or four suppliers on an 'as needed' basis where they find the work and pay an agreed rate for installing. Or they could decide on an element of all three.

It is apparent from the above example that the kitchen fitter would need to contact major builders in the first case to assess the opportunities and that they would need to identify all suppliers in the given area and make contact. In both cases they would need to discuss the rates the companies were willing to pay.

It is worthwhile keeping a record of the names of contacts with notes appended because at a later stage you may want to discuss opportunities with them again.

### Personal services

In similar fashion, a hairdresser or beauty therapist could approach local hotels and offer to visit once a week or be available for two hours every morning or evening.

It often helps to think laterally about the market for services the public want and to search for new niches. This is perhaps a little easier in cities than country towns, but new initiatives are generally well received in most places.

It is, of course, sensible to do some research about the number of hairdressers, barbers, physiotherapists, private tutors, music teachers and other specialist services provided to individuals. The local *Yellow Pages* is a good starting point where it is often possible to count the number of specialists advertising, noting their location and specialisation. The internet is also likely to have more information.

For many of these services, clients are willing to visit private homes. This will help you to determine whether you could set aside a room in your home, fitted out to meet the needs of the services to be provided. Some time will need to be devoted to working out how many people are operating from town centre salons or clinics to determine both the number and the extent to which location might ultimately be of importance as your business develops and expands.

### Professional services

*Yellow Pages* is again a good starting point for counting the number of lawyers, accountants, architects, surveyors, etc. who operate within your area and the extent to which international/national businesses practise within the locality and to give you an immediate feel of what is going on in the area.

Most solicitors work from offices, not necessarily in town centres but, as they typically charge higher hourly rates than most other professionals, most clients expect to meet in offices and where parking is reasonably available. A further feature of their work is that they are constantly meeting clients and hence need reception and secretarial facilities almost immediately.

Other professionals can and do work from their homes, setting aside and equipping a room with appropriate

equipment and necessary tools of trade. At one
time most of the professions regarded advertising as
unethical as professionals were expected to gain clients
through recommendation and reputation although PR
activities were widely used. This ban was lifted during
the latter part of the last century and advertising is now
used even if only in *Yellow Pages*. Some professionals
do still work through recommendation and social
networking, but the majority, however, have some
market presence so can be easily identified.

Professions often cover a wider range of skills than
tradesmen or those offering personal services so it
will probably be necessary to break the market into
segments. A second feature is that they provide services
to the public and to commercial businesses and
sometimes even government bodies. The probability is,
therefore, that you will be able to build a business faster
by offering special services. This does not stop you
attracting other types of work but it helps to be known
for something. I will deal with this strategy more
fully in subsequent chapters, but when gaining market
information it pays to look for gaps in the market and/
or to identify sectors where competition is less intense.

This recommended further analysis is important because
it helps define your business strategy; another subject
I will deal with more fully later on. Providing services
to large organisations is quite different to serving the
general public or even smaller companies. It is ultimately
difficult in business to be all things to all men.

Market analysis is almost certainly more important for professional businesses and links back to the self-analysis recommended early on in this book. The objective is to fit your skills to the right niche.

### Management services

In that market analysis is important for professionals setting up in business, it is vital for individuals wanting to provide their skills to operating businesses. It is equally important that you know both your own skills and attributes and that you are aware of your limitations. The approach here is almost backwards because I suggest you start by defining what you can do and what type of businesses you have worked in.

Let us assume you have worked in manufacturing business only and held a position of responsibility in one large production unit. You have some immediate strengths, including your management background, industry knowledge awareness of all other departmental management roles and how they fit together and how to apply your skills for the common good of the business.

Your principal limitation is that you lack industry knowledge of other types of business – construction, retail, mail order, financial services, etc. It follows that you should limit yourself to manufacturing, at least in the early years and need therefore to identify all the manufacturing companies to whom you could offer your services. In the early stages of your new career this should be companies within easy reach, say under one hour each way as clients will not want to meet expenses for accommodation, etc. You also need to think about the size of business. The probability is that you want to provide your skills to companies who do not have them to a greater or lesser extent, but you want firms who are large enough to need those skills and to afford your fees, say companies with more than £2 million turnover or more than 20 employees. Companies with more than £10 million turnover or a 100 employees may already have formed an internal department, but not always. A reasonable target grouping, therefore, might be manufacturing companies between £2–10 million turnover and not less than 20 employees.

This needs detailed research but the reality of your situation is that you can only realistically supply to a small market, but it is equally true that with as few as 15 clients you might make a satisfactory income whereby you develop longer-term relationships and gradually improve your fee rates.

Dunn & Bradstreet produce *Key British Enterprises* every year, which has considerable information on companies in every sector of the economy. They also have a database that includes significant details about almost every business. They can analyse this into bespoke segments and rent it to you as a mailing list or supply on disc. A company called Jordans offer a similar service. A modest investment in this, if affordable, will save a great deal of work. For instance you might ask D & B to put together a list of all manufacturing companies in Leicestershire, complete with details of directors, company turnover, number of employees, profits and, of course, addresses.

Most providers of individual, expert services to companies could loosely be classified as being in the consultancy field and might have backgrounds in HR, IT, work study, accountancy, marketing, production or commercial art, etc. The potential customers in most of these cases are likely to be businesses in the second stage of their development or moving beyond the entrepreneurial stage, requiring management skills but probably unable to afford hiring their own experts. People with specialist skills could also approach larger firms, but the small business sector definitely lacks wider management skills and a management service of only two days per month could have significant impact within some small businesses.

Further definition is likely to be needed. Trading companies, for instance, might handle £5 million of sales with only three or four people and are, therefore, unlikely to need even a partial HR package. They are likely also to buy standard software packages off the shelf. Such companies, however, could well be interested in re-designing their sales literature or developing an advertising campaign.

For those of you choosing fields of this nature for your business, the market is more specific. Unlike the tradesmen or professionals identified above who need do little more than make their presence known to the general public, you are going to have to approach the market and communicate with individuals in companies who might buy your product or service. The more precisely therefore that you can identify the market the faster you will grow your business. It is well worth approaching specialist companies like Dunn & Bradstreet or Jordans and ask them to design specific packages for you that will identify all companies in the target turnover bracket within your chosen area so that you automatically acquire a database of all prospective customers immediately. To my mind this is an essential tool and I will discuss its uses in later chapters. It requires investment, somewhere between £2,000 and £5,000 according to scale and design but well worth the money. You may then need to look at software packages to help you communicate with your prospective clients.

Some businesses are almost national from inception. This may be true of specialist services, particularly IT products or skills. Most small professional businesses can operate in a local area although I know of one accountancy firm that specialises in dental practices and so has clients all over the country.

Having established a database you can progressively make contact with the companies listed either by writing letters, telephoning, sending emails or a combination of all three. It also pays to keep statistics about the contacts, numbers of meetings arranged and assignments gained because you will inevitably need to improve your use of time as you become busier.

### *Trading, mail order and internet*

This is likely to be a more complex market to define as the range of products is almost infinite so the focus here is initially on the choice of products and how they are used. With limited capital available, however, you are likely to be buying less expensive items more generally used than expensive products for a limited number of buyers. For the latter type of products you would probably want to seek agency opportunities.

Initially you will probably buy job lots of let's say up to £10,000 of products you believe you can sell and, realistically, will be seeking large margins in order to do so. In practice it will be extremely difficult to define this type of market with any geographic precision. More probably you will define it in terms of the product itself, i.e. the market for collectibles, or sporting goods. The better way to evolve a market-related approach to selling these types of products is through a study of the competition and analysis of how the market is served. This will be dealt with more fully in succeeding chapters. There are also several reasons why you cannot gatecrash this type of market, which I will also deal with later. Ideally, this type of business could be started as a second income stream and developed progressively. It is ultimately going to need substantial investment and this will take time to acquire, particularly under current tax structures.

## Specialist businesses and internet

This subject probably merits a book of its own, but also needs to be approached with caution. You can rest assured that every con artist has found out how to use the internet by now. Offers abound as to how to become a millionaire by working only ten minutes a day and invite you to subscribe for specialist systems. Competition is increasing, however, so the businesses with any credibility have to offer 'A money back guarantee'. Some of these are worth pursuing, if only to find out what is going on.

Information publishing is one of the more lucrative businesses in itself, particularly where related to business ideas or finance. There are also several betting tipsters who send out invitations to join their club and obtain inside information.

There are offers about how to trade on financial markets virtually every week, most of them highly priced, with either infallible systems or training programmes on trading foreign exchange (Forex), stocks and shares, commodities and even property. As far as I am able to ascertain, only five per cent of respondents ultimately make satisfactory income through use of systems and training programmes. A further five per cent continue trading, showing a small profit that probably does not justify either their investment or time spent trading. The other 90 per cent drop out altogether having made losses.

A concept called **affiliate marketing** is gaining some credence whereby you can become an agent for almost any product sold via the internet. To do this with any success you need to be able to find your way round the internet and to gain insights into how Google, in particular, and others promote the products and direct 'traffic' to websites. You would need to set up a website of your own that promotes products of your choosing. Logically your product range should be directed at a particular market, for example, health or weight loss. You earn commissions from the original owner or promoter of the product by registering a code with Clique Bank or other specialist bank.

Most of the companies promoting systems or training programmes for this type of activity again advertise that you can do this in ten minutes per day and earn thousands, but neglect to tell you that you have to meet the costs of lodging Adwords with Google and the costs of building your own mailing lists. Nevertheless, this is potentially profitable if fully researched and treated as a whole time business and clearly is a form of **Agency**.

### Setting up an agency

You can become an agent for one or more products but, for practical reasons, you should limit the range and ensure that all are targeted at a similar audience, i.e. you could hardly sell specialist machinery and household products simultaneously. If selling to the public at large you are unlikely to have a product range that also sells to industry, and the approaches are quite different.

Many products are sold to households through agency arrangements and there are variations in the nature of agency agreements. Network or multi-level marketing and party plan type schemes abound but, by nature, are variants of pyramid selling that eventually run out of willing buyers and so are unlikely to provide a lasting career unless you are willing to change the nature of the product at intervals. It is also evident that you need to sell low value products at high volumes to make a living and this can be demanding. When selling higher value products like kitchen installations or life assurance you will probably have to meet partners together, necessitating working anti-social hours.

It is implicit that in selling to the general public anyone can be a buyer and therefore there is little purpose in trying to define the market too precisely. The issues are more about competition and price acceptance and techniques used to develop a customer base. This is also true about mail order and selling via the internet.

When selling as an agent to industry it is worth identifying a market where it makes sense to do so, i.e. if you are selling machinery to bottlers you should attempt to identify all products sold in bottles – milk, beer, wines, spirits, water, etc. and purchase a database of such companies. This can be acquired from the same sources stated above and is unlikely to be expensive as it may well be less than a thousand companies. If, on the other hand, you are selling a more general product such as a computerised planning system to manufacturing companies you might quickly ascertain that 100,000 companies could buy your product.

Establishing a comprehensive database would need significant investment and as a sole trader you cannot

realistically be in touch with 100,000 companies – a
single letter to each of them would cost more than
£50,000 and you would have no practical way of
assessing the value of such a mail-shot. In such cases
I would recommend test marketing. Select perhaps
1,000 companies in one area, determine a strategy for
approaching them, another issue to be discussed later,
and carefully calculate the result of various approaches
and also consider the nature of the respondents'
businesses. You may find the response is weighted
towards one particular industry sector or type of
business such as a high level of component assembly.

Maintaining statistics of contacts, meetings and
conversion rates is again worthwhile for reasons stated
above. It is also interesting to study underlying trends
of progress. Are conversion rates improving as you
improve your telephone technique and confidence in
dealing with prospects?

### Creative and specialist activities
Pure creativity is quite rare and is usually more
vocational than market oriented. Nevertheless, if
serious about business the author or artist should
consider whether they could offer a commercial slant
to their work. For the author there is a long-established
publishing industry, usually approached through
literary agents. These outlets publicise their areas
of interest so could be approached on the basis of a
synopsis for a specific genre publication. The publisher
might express interest subject to inclusion of a topical
element as part of the plot – internet fraud or political

shenanigans. Script-writers and playwrights could approach TV companies on a similar basis. Artists might consider whether they would be happy working as designers or in advertising. If not they could research local art galleries to ascertain what sells best in their various areas or whether they have clients who would like a bespoke painting of their child, dog or garden, etc. Carrying out this work whilst still in employment, before launching on a career could reduce the risk. It is relatively easy to spend a year in creative activities that yield no income.

Inventors and designers have a more complex problem that I will talk about more comprehensively later, but I would encourage all of them to consider the potential market and how it is served before embarking on building prototypes or creating designs. I would also recommend that they consider restricting themselves to products for specific industries that need a steady flow of new products, or where they know production processes are laborious.

## The nature of the buying decision

This, too, is an important aspect of defining a market. There is little complexity in selling services to the general public, particularly if they have invited you to call or turned up at your premises. Their decision, in such cases, is usually one of affordability – some might hesitate at a price of £100 for a hair do or beauty treatment, but would have limited choice if they have a burst pipe or gas leak.

Homeowners and individuals do shop around, however, when wanting something of a durable nature such as a new kitchen or electrical re-wiring. In such cases they will probably ask for both designs and quotations. I will deal with how to handle these situations later but, at the fact-finding stage, the point to recognise is that you are unlikely to obtain an immediate order and this adds to your selling costs, even if only by use of your time which detracts from using it for work that pays.

Repeat purchases of supplies and materials used in production are usually handled by professional buying departments who are experts in playing off competition. If selling such products, you need to know the names of buyers and build this into your database.

### The nature of the products

Capital expenditure, investment or longer-term commitments are usually board decisions, often after being advised by specialists within their businesses – production managers, plant engineers, accountants, etc. – hence you often find the need to identify a number of people within one company who can influence a buying decision if selling equipment to larger organisations. Similar factors may apply in different industries. If selling a product used by the building industry, for instance, you may find the right approach is to sell to architects who specify your product. The builder will then almost automatically buy from you, possibly several months later.

It is essential to think this through in relation to your product or service. The larger the sum involved the longer it will take for a prospective customer to make up their mind. If they are considering installing a new central heating system, or engaging a part-time accountant or IT specialist, they are likely to look at several options and talk to other service providers and may wish to understand in detail precisely what the service consists of or where the pipes will go and how they will be screened. Nevertheless, where the decision will be taken by house-owners who, in general terms, are part of the mass market, they do not need to be personally identified in ascertaining your potential market. Your business strategy will be about ways of inviting the public to contact you.

This is equally true of professional services as well as tradesmen's services although in both cases the market could be widened to include local companies. A solicitor could provide debt collection services or employment contracts. An engineer might offer a routine maintenance service. An electrician could specialise in office lighting. In attempting to serve this wider market you are falling into the loose category of consultant type services where closer market definition will ultimately save you time and money.

The offer of personal or consultancy type services to industry will again be a board or managing director decision where you are providing benefits that will be evaluated. Some companies might want an employer's handbook that clearly sets out a disciplinary procedure and thereby avoids the risk of disaffected former or current employees seeking damages against the company through tribunals. Others may want a computer system that integrates planning and buying procedures and controls stock levels thereby yielding cost savings. It is important to understand the thinking behind decisions to hire your services because it helps to define how you approach prospects.

There is a Chinese proverb: **If you do not know where you are going it does not matter which road you take**. I am fundamentally saying, you must be clear about where you are going. Objectivity is critical to business success. I urge you therefore to determine the approximate size of the market for your chosen product within the likely area of operation and determine what share of this business you aim to capture. This evaluation can be carried out and, indeed, should be carried out, before you commit to self-employment.

If we take the examples used above it is evident that the plumber who ascertains there is plenty of room for a new entrant in his locality can quickly be pulling in close to a six-figure income. The professional accountant or solicitor could rapidly double their former incomes if they too understand their local market. There is, however, one further point of the pre-entry analysis that should be carried out and that relates to competition.

# 5 *Studying competition*

## Services to the public

Most individuals who launch a business that provides their personal skills to the general public are likely to be 'me too' businesses, i.e. Fred is an electrician, me too: Mary is a beauty therapist, me too. You cannot, therefore, charge more than Fred or Mary and might have to charge less if you are to break into the market. You are setting up a business that already exists and thereby increasing the competition in the sector or local area and, therefore, in order to be noticed, you need to differentiate yourself in some way. It would be helpful to ascertain the extent to which other electricians, therapists, plumbers, lawyers, nurses, etc. differentiate themselves.

A quick examination of *Yellow Pages* will show, for instance, that some electricians are content simply to be listed, others have display adverts of varying sizes. Most offer installation, re-wiring, testing, and so on, while others tack on additional features like installing fire alarms or under-floor heating or security systems – clear attempts to be slightly different even if only offering a friendly or emergency service. Solicitors, too, clearly try to specialise, with some focusing on family law and divorce, others on accident and injury and some on business law. It is well worthwhile spending time on trying to find out who is already in the market and what their specialities are.

Most one person businesses are under the radar in that they are unlikely to feature on available databases other than basic listings. It is virtually impossible to ascertain how profitable they are until they grow and incorporate as limited companies and, even then, they file only basic figures. Nevertheless, you will need some commercial information in order to guide you, particularly on one of the most important aspects of your business.

## Pricing

Pricing determines whether or not you can make any real money. Most of you will already have some insights into this, if only because Mrs Jones said: 'You were only here for two hours. I got a bill from your boss for £250 and the tap is still leaking.' If you were only earning £150 a day and made three such visits most days you have a clue what the going rate is. It pays to go beyond this, possibly by making a few telephone calls to enquire about charges. Most sole traders are open about this because they have found out that it is easier to have arguments up front before you start a job than afterwards if you have not yet been paid. You do need to establish what the going rate is, or in some cases, the range of prices charged, before launching. You then need to make an assessment of hours spent on various activities.

## Time and how you use it

The majority of businesses that provide a service use an hourly or daily rate as a basis for charging. In other cases a fixed price may be offered that has been calculated by reference to time estimated to do the work. Where additional components or fittings are supplied as part of the service, they can be marked up modestly as an extra. It follows that how you use time will have a marked influence on your success or otherwise. There is little value in agreeing a call out charge of £50, inclusive of the first half hour on site, if it takes two hours to reach the customer. Travelling is an easy way to diminish your effectiveness. Where possible you need to plan your visits to avoid unnecessary travel although this isn't always achievable, particularly if you provide emergency services.

## Keeping an eye on competitors

How many of your prospective competitors have websites and what do they say about themselves? Are the websites interactive? Examine local newspapers to see if competitors advertise or whether editorials are written about them. Try to determine what they do to be noticed. All these things help to give you a flavour of how the business works. It is likely that all these mediums are being used by solo traders who provide services to the general public. The more advertising and promotion activity you see the more competitive the market is likely to be.

A market price exists for most services in most areas and can usually be ascertained, if not directly then by asking friends to make telephone calls to prospective competitors to find out.

## Services to industry

It is somewhat harder to find out about services sold to industry because you are more likely to find national suppliers who have a wider range of services and an established reputation. In some cases such as a telesales service they fix keen prices, in others such as marketing and strategic planning, consultants could be priced at over £1,000 per day but, as a solo trader, you are unlikely to be able to charge even somewhere close to that. Gaining the knowledge, however, does give pointers.

## Study how the product or service is sold

A further aspect of competition is a consideration of how the product or service is sold. This too is worth a little time and here you can probably find worthwhile information on the internet. How many of your prospective competitors have websites and what do they say about themselves? Are the websites interactive? Does the industry sector you want to enter have agents selling services, or specialist recruitment organisations? If so, consider trying to talk to them about what they do and how they might help you.

You are unlikely to find anything worthwhile in local papers or magazines, if only because it rarely pays to advertise to a small audience that can be reached in other ways. You should, however, look at industry trade journals in the sector you are planning to enter. Apart from ascertaining whether competitors advertise or use PR it will indicate areas of interest to prospective clients.

If contemplating services to particular industry sectors you should also look at the mediums they use to sell to their customers to gain as wide an understanding as possible. The service you provide has to be essential to your customer, in which case he is already buying it, or do something to improve his business or profitability.

### General trading, internet and mail order

This type of business is usually much more concerned with products rather than services and so you can quickly ascertain who your competitors are, how they promote themselves and the media they use and how they use it. The internet has become a shop window where everything is on display, products are described and prices are fully disclosed. EBay is a little different in that it conducts an auction, usually dealing in individual products.

It pays to spend considerable time studying these sources. I would argue it is essential. As a sole trader, operating on your own account you are unlikely to be offering an extensive range initially and must focus on one or two products. You should list everybody you

can find who sells similar products. List their range
and prices, try to examine their product specifications;
draw up a table of comparisons. Study their websites
and try to ascertain the extent to which they use offers,
i.e. 'Three for the price of two'. How else are they
promoting? Go to retailers and see if they offer better
value.

Examine the extent to which competitors use other
media, such as magazines and newspapers. Do adverts
refer readers to their website or sell direct? What aspect
of the product, or special feature, do they promote
hardest? With these types of business I seriously
recommend compiling a comprehensive database about
competitors. The internet is less about generating the
impulse purchase but more about meeting the needs of
the browser looking for the right product at the right
price.

### Agency

Before closing a deal with the intended principal you
should ask them to supply all the information they have
about the market, region or territory that they want you
to work in. It is also important for you to know that
they understand something about the market before
launching out with only good intentions. It may be
that the principal is hiring you because of your market
knowledge in which case their lack of knowledge is less
critical.

Similarly, you should reasonably expect your principal
to know about the competition. Who are they, what

are their product ranges, specifications and prices. This is necessary to help you make an evaluation about your principal's business and its prospects of success in the chosen area and help you identify sub-sections where you are likely to have better opportunities. Agents need to be optimistic and positive but also look at the facts. You will not sell many Ford cars in an area where everyone drives Rolls Royces and vice versa.

# 6 *Specifying your product or service*

I have already stated and want to stress that everything happens in the mind first and that a positive attitude is needed, but positive should not be confused with arrogant, a totally different mindset. It is true that a certain conceit is needed or, more precisely, a belief in oneself. The confidence, however, should be developed through an analysis of the factors likely to affect your business, the setting of objectives, a plan to achieve them, then implementation followed by ongoing monitoring and review. You are unlikely to get everything right straight off, but experience is a great teacher.

## Analysis of the factors

You cannot hope to find out everything you need to know before launching. Indeed, the people who go on trying to obtain all the facts are less likely ever to start a business but, as described in the foregoing chapters, you do need basic information before commitment.

The first consideration is to be honest with yourself about who and what you are. You need to be:

- competent at what you do

- self-reliant

- a reasonable communicator

- able to handle numbers

- capable of developing a positive attitude

- objective.

If you see too many negatives you will subconsciously transmit this to customers and create doubt in their minds. Remember they are looking to you to solve their problems.

You really should make an initial assessment of the market as comprehensively as possible so that you have a background picture of what is going on. Some of you will list everything you find out or even build a computerised record. Others will trust memory. It pays to be disciplined, but the longer you run a business the more you will know about the market and competition, and you will, of course, bring your own knowledge and experience into the equation, but you do have to make an early decision about whether there is room enough in the market for you to enter.

If the answer is yes, the next question is how can you differentiate yourself from competitors or, if not, can you survive as me too? This does require some study, even if only *Yellow Pages*, reading all the adverts, trying to determine if a particular aspect of the service is not well covered or, alternatively, is there a service you are particularly good at or understand thoroughly. Be conscious at all times that you are trying to position yourself in the market to be noticed by potential customers.

## Setting objectives

I will deal with financial objectives and considerations in a subsequent chapter. This section is more about defining your position in the market and your outline business strategy.

We have talked about studying the competition, as far as reasonably possible, to understand where their focus is and more particularly to determine if there is some ground they do not appear to cover. Finding a niche in most markets is an attractive thing to do for two reasons. In the first place it provides an opportunity to break into the market if you can fill the niche. Second, you can become known for a particular service where competition is less severe and so progressively increase prices and profitability as well as becoming more expert and efficient through repetition. When starting up you will probably undertake every chance you get to build your business. However, a degree of specialisation in a particular service or on a market sector often brings higher rewards and helps you launch sooner.

# Skilled trades

As stated earlier most trades are essentially 'me too' businesses, i.e. a plumber is a plumber, a carpenter is a carpenter, but this should not prevent you from looking for an edge or something extra you can add. A plumber might advertise: 'New bathrooms a speciality' or a carpenter: 'Re-organise your bedroom with fitted cupboards'.

It is implicit in both cases that if you can rip out and fit a new bathroom you can obviously replace a leaking tap or burst pipe, or fix shelves. You do not need a whole essay about what else you can do. A word of caution, however, as most customers will want a total product, not just the bare bones, i.e. they do not want merely a new sink, lavatory and bath and be left to tile the walls and redecorate the room themselves, or to paint the wardrobes.

This clearly implies that you must think through precisely what you offer so that you optimise on your time and skills. It follows that unless you are a complete handyman you will fare no better than the ordinary DIY performer. If, therefore, you intend to offer a full service you must team up with other professionals, even if only informally. A dissatisfied customer is damaging to your reputation and reputation is often of paramount importance in these fields.

As part of gaining a background awareness of the market, we touched on the possibility of working with builders on housing sites and/or with jobbing builders on smaller projects. It follows that choice therefore exists as to how to position yourself and, implicit in such positioning is that it imposes limitations. If engaged on building sites it would be slightly absurd for an electrician to offer an emergency service that he would not have a hope of fulfilling. It may mean that offers of work sometimes have to be declined, which is hard to do in the early stages of building a business, but you cannot ultimately be all things to all men and must therefore make a choice and stick to it.

I will elaborate further on this when discussing marketing later in Chapter 8, but I do want to stress, at this stage, that part of the purpose of the information gathering stage is to both seek niches that you can fill in the marketplace and to be clear about what you offer. It is of course implicit that a qualified and experienced tradesman is able to carry out most of the jobs expected within the trade description.

The specification of a one person business is largely about defining yourself in your chosen field in a way that should be easily noticed and, preferably one that sets you apart from your competitors. This is, of course, often difficult as you will be immediately recognised by your core skill – plasterer, chimney sweep, roofer, etc. This definition alone implies coverage of services expected to be provided under such generic terms and this is often enough to become noticed and to attract work of a general nature, but you are only one of a list of names to a customer researching a particular service.

It will probably pay to add or stress a particular skill. These simple definitions help you to be noticed or to look that little bit different but do not try to stress too many things. By emphasising a particular expertise you are merely trying to be noticed. It will not exclude you from other services expected to be provided by a tradesman, but if the customer wants the specific service you have mentioned you may be able to set a fixed price that is more attractive than an hourly rate.

## Personal services

This sector, too, has much in common with trades although, in many ways, the generic terms are even more defining but the same criteria apply. A music teacher, for instance, could elaborate further. Do you merely give piano lessons or do you cover other instruments? Do you distinguish between classical and popular or other types of music?

Do you have any special skills as a chiropractor? Do you offer a massage service? Can you immediately locate and define the cause of pain? Are you a hair stylist with knowledge of historic styles – the 1940s, 50s, etc? Have you ever worked for a celebrity?

As a teacher, do you work with specific age groups and do you prefer to teach groups or individuals? What are your best subjects – languages, literature, maths and sciences, history, etc?

In all cases you are looking for that extra edge that helps you to be noticed and in defining yourself you are also defining your market and the chosen skills you will be most happy applying. In the early stages you may feel you are limiting yourself, but there is no reason why you should not take work with which you are identified as a therapist or trainer, but you will ultimately be more successful by doing the work you most prefer.

## Professional services

This has been partially dealt with already in that professionally qualified people cover a wider range of activities than most people who offer trade skills or personal services. Specialisation ultimately becomes a necessity for most professionals. While one expects a lawyer to know something about most aspects of the law it is a rare solicitor who can deal simultaneously with clients whose problems range from criminal charges for offences to boundary disputes with neighbours to residence issues over children whose parents are divorcing and a builder who has planning issues with the local council.

Several lawyers do attempt to do this and find stimulus in dealing with a wide range of problems, but their limitations are often exposed when issues come to Court and specialists are involved.

Similarly, most surveyors tend to specialise in building projects and management or valuations of houses and effects or planning issues. Accountants, too, specialise as auditors or tax consultants or providers of book-keeping services and architects become known for house extensions or pub refurbishments or private clinics.

Once more the chosen specialisation defines them and their market sector and as project managers, tax consultants or criminal lawyers they also fall into the 'me too' category and need an additional edge to help define them further to ensure they are noticed.

A family lawyer might therefore call themselves a specialist in divorce and arbitration. An accountant might define themselves as: 'a tax consultant specialising in tax planning for retirement'. It is implicit in both cases that they understand family law or taxation issues but, by stating a further expertise, they draw attention to themselves without limiting themselves in their chosen markets.

## Services to commercial undertakings

This sector requires specific definition because you are dealing directly with professionals rather than laymen but, even so, promoting yourself to people who may not consider they have a problem and may be viewing you as somebody who might be able to bring an ultimately commercial benefit to their organisation. This is a far more difficult task than dealing with somebody who has sought you out because they have a specific problem. This type of situation places greater emphasis on your communication skills and you must therefore be confident about what you have to offer as well as gaining an insight into how your potential client's business works so that you can define precisely how your particular skill can blend with the rest of the team.

It is implicit that as a former human relations manager, for instance, you understand something about staff recruitment, job specifications and employment law and probably negotiating with trade unions. The first point to recognise, however, is that you are not seeking a job, rather providing a specific service. This, of course, raises a further question: what service and for whom? The answer, in this case, is probably for a company who does not have a personnel manager or department, implying that the business is not large enough to require a whole-time professional, but likely to have a partial need – a company with say more than 20 employees.

From this simplistic definition some deductions could be made. The company is unlikely to need a professional recruitment service or a union negotiator. There is, however, a probability that it has little knowledge of employment law, sickness benefits or disciplinary procedures and this is a potential entry point. Indeed, with a little research, you might well find several hundred companies, within a reasonable radius of where you live, to whom you could offer this service. You could almost stereotype the format of an employees' handbook on computer so that you are able to customise it for individual clients. Once agreed with the company you could produce professional-looking booklets by using a print on demand service who could print say 50 copies for little over £100.

This service could almost be packaged and offered, complete with a presentation to board members, for a little over one thousand pounds. This would provide you with two benefits. Constant repetition would improve your efficiency and make the service profitable. The professional-looking end product would enhance your credibility and improve your chances of providing further HR services to clients.

An individual IT consultant faces a different set of problems in that so many 'off the shelf' products already exist. This does offer the opportunity, nevertheless, to specialise in installing such systems to smaller companies and providing a back-up service to ensure the client understands the process and uses it efficiently. An alternative is to work for larger companies, offering to develop bespoke systems where substantial fees could be demanded as you are likely to be working at the front end of technology development and you would need to spend considerable time understanding the client's business, what they want and how it would integrate with other systems. The rewards could be rich but it is a difficult market for a sole trader to break into unless you can demonstrate a track record of developing and installing similar type systems.

The point here, however, is that as with the HR consultant you need to pick an area of activity on which you can focus such as development of websites where companies can display all their products, specifications and prices with the facility to add and/or amend from time to time. Again, research will be necessary to identify potential users, and careful consideration should be given as to how best to approach them.

**The underlying message is the same for all one person start ups: try to differentiate yourself from competition by finding the little add on or specialisation that draws attention to you and try to find a niche.**

## Agency, general trading, internet and mail order

Under this heading you are more likely to be dealing with products rather than services but, again, needing to differentiate the product from competitive offerings in the market. In thinking about the features of the product, apply what I call the 'so what' test, i.e.

| | |
|---|---|
| Feature: | It comes readily assembled. |
| So what? | |
| Benefit: | It's ready for immediate use |
| Feature: | It has a high powered motor |
| So what? | |
| Benefit: | Performs more efficiently with less risk of breakdown |

This simple technique helps to define the product's potential appeal to the customer. This should be further refined by matching the features and benefits against competition, again to help differentiate your product. The high powered motor is of less benefit if a competitor has an even more powerful motor. By defining every feature as a benefit and comparing against competitors' offers you should be able to identify differences and evaluate their worth. If they don't add up to much you probably have the wrong product or, conversely, you have something you can stress in the marketplace that will generate sales.

Identifying differences between products is an important sales and marketing technique, particularly where you can lay stress on the benefit derived from such small differences and promote those differences.

I remember many years ago that Unilever produced a washing powder called Omo which was heavily promoted on television under the slogan 'Omo adds brightness' with a caption, Omo with WM7. This was obviously stressing an extra additive around which the advertisers created both a difference and a mystery, which made an ordinary washing detergent one of the best selling brands in the market. WM7 was simply the seventh whitening material the R & D department had experimented with, but this small difference was brilliantly exploited.

# 7 *A different approach for creative ideas*

The truly creative person is in a different position to most individuals wanting to start a business in that they are discussing something that doesn't already exist. Even so it has to find a place in the market and will fall into a general category, i.e. a novel or play is obviously creative and does not yet exist but clearly competes with other works of fiction and, in that sense, cannot be seen as completely unique. The same is true of inventions and designs. Virtually all of them do a job that is already being done in one form or other and so would be seen as substitutes or improvements and be evaluated accordingly. It follows that some market research is therefore essential to test the validity of the idea and ascertain whether it has a place in the market.

With literary works there is a long established practice of bringing them to market through the publishing industry or, in some cases, directly on to radio or TV. The initial approach is usually, but not necessarily, through agents who know where to place such work, but it is a precarious process. Relatively few first novels or plays are published each year and the procedure is time consuming. It could well be two to three years, and often longer, from starting to write to publication so, for most aspiring writers of plays, novels, poetry, etc., it is almost essential to start as a part-time occupation and accept that it will take several years to become established.

In more recent times we have seen growth in self-publishing and use of the internet as a promotional medium and individual copies of books can be produced at quite low cost but, for most producers, the difficulty is in marketing the finished product without a means of gaining support from the retail industry.

For people with a craving to write, markets exist for communicating special skills, knowledge or expertise on specific subjects. Publishers of technical subjects can be approached with merely an outline or synopsis to demonstrate how the subject will be covered, supported by a couple of sample chapters to indicate style and competence. Advances can be secured with this approach, based on the publisher's estimate of likely sales. Freelance writing for journals and magazines can also generate income and, if this field is of interest, the market could be researched quite readily by identifying magazines that deal with your chosen subject and approaching them direct.

Actors and musicians usually follow a vocation and most embark on formal training at an early age in schools of music or acting academies. For most it is implicit that by following such a vocation they will be self employed and probably rely on agents to promote them. They differ from most one person businesses in this respect, but several chapters of this book could still be of value.

Inventors divide into two categories – those who are producing something completely new and those who are seeking a different process or product to replace something that already exists. The probability is that something entirely new falls into the product category as any new process is likely to be a substitute. It should, therefore, be subjected to critical questions:

- What purpose does it serve?

- What need does it satisfy?

- How will it be used?

- Who will use it?

- Does it compete with products of a different nature?

- How large is the ultimate market?

- How will the product be delivered to the market?

- Who are the main players in the market?

- Can the invention be protected by patents or copyright?

If we take something like the original cat's eye we can see how it answered all the questions and posed others.

- It indicates the middle of the road ahead in the dark by reflection in a car's headlights.

- It improves safety for night-time drivers.

- It will be embedded in the road as a permanent feature.

- The Ministry of Transport will specify it for the benefit of road users.

- The alternative is to paint white lines, but they lack the longer range reflective quality.

- The ultimate market is every road in the world at 'say' 300 studs per mile.

- The product must be manufactured and sold to road builders.

- The invention can be patented and protected by an immediate application. The ultimate cost of worldwide patent and trade-mark protection is, however, significant; likely to be in excess of £100,000 in today's money.

The investment required to manufacture immediately rules out the inventor from considering handling this aspect of the project themselves. It is self-evident that it has to be brought to market as quickly as possible, but how?

## Bringing creative ideas to market

The inventor could approach the Ministry of Transport direct but, if in those days it was anything like today, you could be tied up by bureaucracy until after the patent application expires so you are likely to be looking for road-builders to take out territorial licences whereby they would pay an upfront sum, out of which you bear the cost of full patents, plus an ongoing royalty. In this particular case you can see that even a penny per cat's eye would yield millions of pounds. In today's market you would probably back this up with marketing and PR to create public support for the concept. Alternatively you could arrange a licensing agreement with one or more producers.

(I don't know how Percy Shaw, who invented the cat's eye, brought it to market but it typifies the criteria needed for introducing a new concept. Like most things the original concept was quickly modified and improved by other inventors and/or designers.)

For the creators of most new products, however, the probability is that it will replace or improve something that already exists. The same questions used in the above example are still relevant but need expanding to take in how it compares with the existing product(s), the additional features and benefits described in earlier chapters and the comparative costs.

For inventors and designers in this category the only thing you have of value is the concept; you are most unlikely to have the skills to develop a production unit and marketing campaign. The investment cost is also likely to be significantly ahead of what sole traders could reasonably afford, and seeking third party investment into a concept is virtually a non-starter unless you have a competent management team with a track record.

In this sense I come back to the comments made in Chapter 3 – know yourself and your limitations. If you are a truly creative person do not dissipate your talents by taking on management responsibilities you are not qualified to handle. Confine yourself to determining the value of the concept by:

- ascertaining how it fits into the market

- the competitive advantages of your product or design

- assessing the value of the existing market for the existing competitive product and estimate the extent to which an improved product could extend it

- identifying the producers/marketers of the existing product and their likely reaction to a new competitive product

- finding out how many other companies supply complementary products and which of them would welcome an extension to their range

By these means you will define companies who could bring your product/concept/design to market and put yourself in a position to structure an approach to them to negotiate a licensing agreement or outright sale. Alternatively, and provided you are satisfied your concept has genuine commercial value, you could invite either an accountant or marketing agency to assist with negotiations for a fee or commission. Personally, if I was brought into assisting with negotiations, I would want to see comprehensive answers to the above questions before accepting the brief and would expect to charge for researching any deficiencies.

With designs and inventions one also has to consider the likely 'shelf-life'. Where substituting established products it is likely to have a reasonable life cycle, but fashion products or designs are unlikely to last for as much as five years. Some industries seek new products competitively and several designers and inventors focus on them. The fashion industry is an obvious one but the toy industry is constantly seeking new products or add-ons to existing brands. Industries using packaging frequently seek design change, particularly cosmetics and confectionery. Life cycles are short, however, so royalty yields rarely gross six figures in total. Nevertheless, there is merit in focusing on particular industries and becoming recognised as a specific type of inventor or designer.

By doing so you will come to understand the industry's needs and tailor your concepts accordingly and you will eventually become known to the companies seeking new products, embellishments and/or designs and thereby have immediate access to present your ideas. Many successful businesses have been built by package designers, fashion designers and product inventors that rely on producing a stream of designs or products rather than seeking the one invention that makes their fortune. Such businesses can also benefit by utilising the guidelines discussed above.

# 8 *Marketing*

It is obvious that once you start up in business you need
to become known to your potential customers and must
therefore consider advertising in one form or another
in order to promote your skills and services. Costs have
to be restricted, of course, because the money is not
available.

## Skilled trades

You probably need to advertise in *Yellow Pages* and area
telephone directories, but these are produced annually
and it may therefore be several months before your
advertisements are seen.

It may be worthwhile approaching a local newspaper
and to try to persuade it to write an article about
you. To achieve this, however, you will need to have
something different to say. It is insufficient to suggest
there are too few carpenters in Bristol so I have set
up on my own to help fill the gap. It might be more
interesting to say that you produce modern replicas of

Georgian furniture to an equivalent standard to the craftsmen of that era, particularly if you can back this with photographs.

You might also consider printing a leaflet for insertion in the local newspaper and also building a website. Some research on the internet will identify designers, and a decent website can be put together for as little as £250. In doing so, remember that the internet and websites are visual mediums, i.e. a picture tells a thousand words. Messages should be punchy rather than grammatical. If you adopt this suggestion, try to ensure that visitors to your site are able to leave a message and be sure to call them back or reply at the first chance you have.

The internet is becoming an increasingly important medium for promoting business. With the advent of Google Local it is possible to be listed on Google's local page service without paying for adwords and, indeed, you do not necessarily need a website as Google will hold a page of details, including photographs, that browsers may instantly refer to and thereby obtain details about your service immediately.

In Chapter 7 I talked about differentiating yourself so that you can stress these messages in advertising and image building. The most important communication, however, is a job well done. Thereafter you can reasonably ask your client or customer to recommend you to friends and associates.

I also recommend keeping records of what you have done for clients or customers and building your own database and sending occasional messages to them to remind them you are still in business. This helps to build goodwill and if people are well disposed towards you they will recommend you to others.

Advertising and promotion will probably seem expensive to most people starting up and almost all of you will be disappointed with returns. It therefore pays to be absolutely clear about how you present yourself to the outside world and the more you can make your audience think of you as bringing something new and valuable to the market, the faster your business will take off. The major advertisement is to do a good job as smartly and efficiently as possible. Talk to your customers. Tell them you are starting out and would appreciate referrals. Ask your friends to recommend you – make sure you leave a business card with contact details everywhere you go.

### Selling the benefits

In order to put your message across effectively you need to try to visualise yourself as your potential customer and ask the question: What do they really want?

Bearing in mind that you might be facing competition sooner or later you should try to think about the particular advantages your customer wants. What is likely to please them most about you? Customers want to understand how they will **benefit** from buying your product or service. Always try to think about the advantages your customer will derive by using your service. This is relatively easy when the customer has called you in or sought you out in order to find a solution to their immediate problem but more difficult when it becomes evident they have spoken to competitors.

By concentrating on benefits you will put a positive picture in your customer's mind. If an electrician describes how they are going to chip all the plaster off the wall to bury the cable, the customer will focus inevitably on the mess they will create. It is far better to say that you will fit discreet power points adjacent to the TV and Hi-fi, rather than trail electric cable across the room. If you do have to make a negative statement, perhaps in answer to a question, be sure to counter its effect immediately: 'Well yes, it is expensive, but look what you get for it . . .'

### Dealing with competition

You will not win every time but unless you are constantly thinking about how to match and beat competition you might lose every time. It pays to keep an ear to the ground to help find out if any competitor is doing something different or has a cheaper source of supply if you are also providing fitments or relatively expensive components that give them an edge. It is important to have done your homework, as stated in Chapter 4, so that you know the areas in which competitors specialise and to keep this information up to date. In part you carried out this exercise in order to try and differentiate yourself in the marketplace. You should use this knowledge to stress these differences in terms that appeal to your customer, particularly if at a price disadvantage, i.e. 'The reason Smith and Jones are cheaper is because they plan to erect a pole and run the cable across the garden like a clothesline whereas I plan to encase it in conduit and sink it underground alongside the garden path. You won't know it's there, but you"ll always be able to find it.'

Try to avoid overtly knocking competition unless they are widely known to do shoddy work. Even then it is better to put a question in the customer's mind by damning with faint praise. 'Oh yes, they are in and out fast but always seem to be busy if you have any problems with the installation later.' The seed of doubt is likely to grow, particularly if you make your story convincing but do not use phrases like superior quality. It is better to say: 'You won't have any trouble when I have finished, and I can put you in touch with other customers I have worked for.' This approach stresses the benefit of no hassle and reinforces the previous statement that they might have hassle with the competitor. It also implies that the customer should check you both out and that he is likely to obtain good references about your work and adverse comment about your competitor.

## Personal services

The promotional activities you need to carry out are similar in many ways to those described above for tradesmen. It is usually worthwhile to be listed in

*Yellow Pages* and local directories as soon as possible and to attempt to gain press comment or articles about your new business activities or dropping leaflets round housing estates saying who you are.

It is equally true that you need satisfied customers who can be induced to recommend you, so business cards are a useful prompt to be handed out. Websites nowadays are virtually a must, particularly where you can use photographs of clients freshly made up or with smart new hairdos. This may be of less value to teachers or nurses, but still can be turned to advantage with images of smiling children who have passed their exams, or before and after pictures of somebody bent double who has been helped to stand up. A little creative thinking can take you forward quite quickly.

Again, in dealing with customers, remember to sell the benefits. For instance, if you provide a tailoring service or sell clothing, the emphasis should be on how the customer looks in them. 'It fits beautifully on you and makes you look quite slim', has more impact than, 'the cloth was produced by one of the best mills in Yorkshire and the jacket is hand stitched'. The first statement has emotional appeal; the second is factual and may reinforce the earlier message once the customer has decided they look good in the outfit. It can be quite important to add the reinforcement message so that the customer can go home and explain to their partner that it was an absolute bargain because the material comes from one of the best mills in Yorkshire . . .

This type of image painting is, of course, an obvious approach for hairdressers and beauty therapists but can also be used by chiropractors or medical service practitioners with comments like: 'Improved posture and fluent movements really do help you look so much younger and more attractive than hobbling along . . .'

By making customers feel good about themselves you can be reasonably sure of repeat visits and recommendations and of building your own reputation. Word of mouth is by far the best and least expensive way to build your business and will help you raise prices, possibly ahead of competition.

## Professional services

I have talked quite a lot about trying to differentiate yourself from competitors when setting up in business in order to become noticed. This could be further exploited in promoting your business activities by clever use of PR. Most professions are made up of people with well above average intelligence who have passed demanding exams and, in doing so, gained a wealth of knowledge which they have added to with experience. They should therefore be able to write fluently about aspects of their services and experience in an interesting manner. For those professionals wanting to build a local practice they could meet the local newspaper editors and offer to produce a weekly or monthly column covering varied aspects of their service.

A lawyer, for instance, might write an occasional review of family case law, an accountant might write

about dealings with the Inland Revenue or a doctor
might write about latest breakthroughs in medicine
or progress with research into diseases and treatment.
Many local papers would welcome this type of
contribution, particularly if free and it is, of course, free
advertising for the local professional who is displaying
some measure of expertise.

A website is likely to be of benefit but needs a great
deal of creativity to make interesting pictorially, but is
worth a try. A folder with leaflets about services can be
produced for modest cost and could be used as a mail-
shot to prospective clients and, indeed, as the client
base grows, a periodic newsletter is a helpful way of
keeping in touch with clients and prompting them to
recommend your services.

As with all services to people, satisfied clients are
your best advertisement and handling them with skill
is important. Like everybody else you should also be
selling the benefits of using your service. An accountant
might suggest that by setting up a company you will
save at least £3,000 a year in National Insurance costs,
or an insurance broker might say that by making a will
and taking out a life policy it will pay the Inheritance
tax when you die. Talk about results and effects rather
than how you will carry out the work.

## Services to industry

For those of you intending to provide your skills to
industrial customers you almost certainly need to
acquire some sort of database of potential clients,

ideally one that provides names of specific personnel to whom you can write or speak to on the telephone. Eventually you need to sit in front of a decision maker in the companies approached and will need to put your message over crisply and be able to answer any questions posed.

I know very few people who enjoy 'cold calling', and many people positively hate it. If this applies to you then you could brief a telesales agency to sell the product direct, but a service will almost certainly require personal contact so ask them to set up meetings with identified people on your database. The telesales message should be scripted together with answers to frequently asked questions.

You could consider a mail-shot describing your service, in which case I suggest you stagger the postings, say 50 per week, followed by a personal call or telesales call designed to obtain a meeting. If you opt for this technique it helps to keep statistics. You might find that out of every 100 letters you are only able to talk to 60 people subsequently, but only five agree to meet you. Thereafter only one commissions an assignment. This would actually be a good return in a start up situation. If you obtain three assignments per 1,000 letters backed by telephone calls and meetings you would be doing quite well. The response to mail-shots that are not followed up is likely to be less than one per 1,000.

By keeping statistics of this nature you can work out how much it costs to obtain one client and, equally important, ascertain what you need to do to obtain one client.

You may find, for instance, that printing 1,000 leaflets costs £100 or 10p each, postage and envelopes 60p each and telesales calls at 20p each. You can quickly see that it has cost £900 in cash to obtain one client and you may have to spend one day per week coordinating the activity. Clearly, if each assignment yields only two days work at £400 per day, the cost of marketing is too high and you may be obliged to cut out literature and postage and spend a day a week on the phone yourself.

Statistics about how you spend your time and money are important in a one person business, particularly where you are trying to break into company accounts. It is also well worthwhile knowing how you spend your time when serving the public.

Winning the business from other businesses must be done face to face if you are to provide a service. The managing director will almost certainly want to interview you, not only to ascertain that you are competent in the service you provide, but also to ensure that you understand their problems and that you will fit in with the people in their team. If, as in the above example, it costs £180 merely to gain a meeting it will pay you to learn as much as you can about the company and the person you are meeting beforehand. Study the company's website. At the very least it will describe the company's products and services and probably describe the directors' backgrounds.

The meeting is the most important element of your marketing plan. You must, therefore, be in control of the agenda. We each have individual styles. Personally I find it helpful to ask lots of questions. Managing directors like to talk about their businesses and what they are trying to do with it. In doing so, they frequently expose their problems, thereby guiding you towards opportunities to help improve things by using your skills. It helps, too, if you appear relaxed and authoritative and throw in the odd anecdote to reinforce that you have dealt with similar problems before, but do not do too much of the talking.

Conversations roll along quite easily, particularly in the private sector where the likelihood is that the person you are talking to founded the business and is proud of their achievement. By letting them talk and by throwing up questions that indicate you know what you are talking about you plant seeds that will germinate in their mind. If we refer back to an earlier example of an ex HR manager, they might ask: 'Has any former employee taken you to a tribunal?' and then add, 'Messy business, takes up days of your time.' Such a question immediately implies that you know something about tribunals and diverts your prospect to talking about the subject you want to discuss more fully. You are then able to lead into how you can avoid them with a clearly defined disciplinary procedure and an employees' handbook. The well-targeted question puts you back in control of the meeting.

As in all self-promotion type discussions you have to sell benefits and, in this situation, you might do this by describing the downside for the client with comments like, 'I had a client recently who had a stroppy foreman he wasn't getting along with too well so he sacked him in a fit of pique one day.' With a shake of the head, continue, 'If he thought he had problems before he soon learned they were only just beginning . . .'

The tale of horror proceeds and culminates with, 'He could have avoided all this aggro by investing as little as twelve hundred pounds.'

The benefits are implicit in this type of presentation, and the short anecdote enhances them in the client's mind. You might even add, 'It only needs one tribunal and you have blown at least ten times that amount.'

The advantage of this approach is that you are displaying knowledge and experience without appearing to be pushy and you are putting yourself on equal terms with the customer sitting opposite. It is now relatively easy to lead into, 'Three days of my time and the problem is solved. Not only that, you finish up with a glossy booklet to hand out to all your staff and that helps them to feel good about you.'

Fear is usually a quicker motivator than reward and if used in a casual manner can generate action, particularly where your package is succinct and easy to understand.

I should stress here that you do not need to be extrovert to conduct this type of meeting. It pays to be tidily dressed, confident about what you are able to do and relaxed and at ease with yourself. Try not to be anxious or dominating.

Similar techniques can be applied by accountants, IT managers, marketers, buyers and so on. It does help to try and build a package you can offer rather than a more abstract service and to think through the benefits to the client and reasons why they should agree to purchase your service.

Competition clearly exists in this sector but less frequently from individuals providing a particular management service. There is, however, a well-established market for management consultants, but usually aimed at larger corporations than I am recommending for start up, one person businesses. Such practices are unlikely to be seeking small, short-term assignments, however, so competition should not be a serious factor in this sector in the early stages of your new career.

## Sales agents

By its very nature agency is primarily about selling either to the general public or to corporations. As an agent selling to the public it is reasonable to expect the principal, who owns the product or has rights thereto, to understand and identify the market and to provide promotional services whether through advertising, PR, mailing and/or other activities. The company may or may not provide the leads. If not, you are in a similar position to people selling services and almost everything stated in that section above will apply here.

Similarly, if selling to corporations, as an agent with little or no back-up, you have identical requirements to people selling their services to corporations and should make contact as described above and progressively build a database of prospects and customers. The communication process and need for statistics is virtually the same for products as for services if handled through agency agreements.

It is implicit that people from a sales background are professional communicators and have acquired a style whereby they pass the odd friendly remark to receptionists and secretaries, dress smartly and comport themselves in a manner that helps them to be recognised and remembered. Selling benefits should be second nature and conducting meetings with clients a fundamental part of their day-to-day experience. It is therefore reasonable to believe that most will already have evolved a personal style, and therefore launching themselves should be far less intimidating than for accountants or IT managers or those who are more likely to be of an introvert nature.

The principal issues for agents are about their products and about arranging meetings. Product analysis compared with competitive products has already been discussed so that you are able to highlight the features and define the benefits.

In most cases of operating a single person agency the product defines the market, with one or two exceptions. Household products and services, or supplying the public at large is, of course, a mass market so it would be reasonable to expect your principal to advertise to attract leads. On the other hand, with products like life assurance, you may obtain an occasional lead through company general advertising and mail-shots but would expect to generate the bulk of your business through personal contacts and networking and, indeed, products such as pensions could be sold to companies. This situation will probably oblige you to choose one market or other. You can see companies in the daytime and possibly individual managers employed by them whereas personal contacts must be seen out of office hours.

For the agent who has a product likely to be used exclusively by specialist companies, say labelling equipment that could apply labels to bottles, packages and cans, the process is one of research to build a database of likely customers – food canners, cosmetic and toiletry companies, bottling businesses, etc. You would probably need to know the names of a few people within the identified target companies – production managers, chief engineers, technical buyers – and aim to speak to all of them. Again, you should study prospects' websites before contacting them so that you have some knowledge in order to start discussions.

In cases like this, requiring capital expenditure, the decision to buy will be taken by the board, based on recommendations and advice from within the management team so, when a decision is pending, a major objective should be to try to arrange a formal presentation to everybody who could influence the final choice. This should be carefully planned with either videos or power point projections and handouts to leave behind. The commission on the sale could be rather large.

For products that could be used by almost any company, say coffee machines, you might set up a database of all local companies, possibly 2–3,000 and make contact either directly by phone or set up meetings through a telesales operator. This type of product, while less expensive than capital equipment, is nevertheless a one-off purchase and therefore unlikely to be handled in the first instance by the company buyer. The initiative might be taken by whoever is responsible for running the canteen and tea service. A better approach with this type of product might be direct to the managing director or their secretary and ask who would handle the matter within his organisation.

In all cases, where selling to industry customers, I do strongly recommend the acquisition and use of a database with company name, address, website and names of executives likely to be concerned with the purchase of the product you are selling.

# General trading, internet and mail order

It is implicit in the heading that most of your communication will be written and that advertising, in one form or another, has a major part to play. It is also highly probable that you are dealing with physical products or 'packaged' services, i.e. seminars or writing courses or guides on a particular topic.

The first question that must be answered is can you identify the target markets and, if so, can you locate them? If you are selling to the general public you have less of a problem but for more specific products, sports equipment, filing cabinets or anti-ageing capsules, the more closely you can identify potential buyers, the greater the returns. In such cases you might try small adverts in specialist magazines where your product would be of interest to readers. This could be a short advert referring interested parties to your website for a bigger display that invites direct response either to a warehouse or fulfilment service.

A particular objective of these types of operations is to build a database progressively of people who have bought your products or something similar. In this way you can mail details of new products to them with the probability that a greater proportion of recipients will take up the offer.

There are brokers who provide mailing lists, usually for rent, but any respondents belong to you once they become customers. You could join internet groups where personal details are provided and add members who are likely to fall within your target group to your database, i.e. everybody above 50 might be a buyer of anti-ageing cream or stop hair loss products. It is not precise but it has a greater probability of evoking a higher response than mailing to the masses. The build up of a database of customers who buy from time to time is a paramount objective of most mail order businesses.

In the modern world a website is an essential tool. Many potential buyers will look you up to try to ensure you are a credible supplier. More importantly it is an aid for cutting costs. You could, for instance, advertise discounted golf clubs for sale as a one liner in a national newspaper that refers readers to your website where you have full product descriptions, complete with benefits and prices and invites them to place an order immediately. The point is that you have minimised advertising costs. By referring to your website it is implicit they do not have to make a commitment, but the website hits them with a presentation that says so much more than an advert. It also gives greater comfort in that a detailed specification is made available which helps the prospect consider where they might locate the product in their home or garden, or demonstrates how it is used.

A well-designed website helps sales. Make yours as customer friendly as possible to enable a browser to call up the range of products they are interested in possibly buying, allowing them to choose from the range, readily access detailed descriptions and leading them naturally to the order page and credit card details.

There is a skill in writing good copy in a user friendly way, or designing adverts that appeal. If you do not have these skills, hire the services of somebody who does. It need not be expensive and will pay for itself several times over.

Again, with this type of business, I want to stress the importance of keeping statistics. Set your website up in such a way that the browser has to use the password gleaned from the advertisement they have recently looked at. Monitor the number of hits from each password so that you can evaluate the response from each advert. Set up a different password for each email sent to your database and yet another for each mail-shot. Check the response from each. Your aim is to notify the maximum number of prospective purchasers at the lowest possible cost and obtain the highest response pro rata to the number of mailings or emails. Clearly emails will be the lowest cost but usually need supplementing with advertising or other promotion to keep building a database of potential buyers. If you can hone down advertising, mailing and promotional costs and ultimately achieve a 2 per cent order response rate you will have a durable and profitable business.

## Creative people

At some point in the creative process you need to be in touch with end users, promoters or distributors of the

type of products you are creating. Such contact needs
delaying until you are part way through the creative
process and certain of achieving a finished product
– a novel, prototype or collection of poems. Nobody
is going to enthuse and talk money about mere ideas
unless you have a strong track record.

For producers of written works – novels, plays, poetry,
film scripts, etc., the *Artists' and Writers' Yearbook* is an
invaluable guide. It lists literary agents and publishers in
the UK, America and other English speaking territories,
giving names of the people whom you should contact
and what they would like to see, to help them
determine whether to take a deeper look at what you
have to offer, and how you should approach them. You
should follow these guidelines as most people do not
have the time to read an unsolicited novel of 500 pages.

Most agents already have a client list of published
authors, playwrights and poets that usually includes
famous names, and they are busy people with little
time to spend on proposals from unknown writers.
They are likely to deal with material sent to them
superficially unless something grabs their attention.
Your covering letter should therefore be succinct, but
say what is exciting and/or different about your work
and the synopsis and sample chapters/scenes/poems
must demonstrate your ability and be of immediate
interest. Be warned, agents take on very few new clients
each year. The advantage in using their services and
paying their commissions is that they know where best
to place your work and are experienced negotiators.

Publishers can be approached direct and are receptive to new ideas. Their first consideration, particularly with new writers, is about the market for the publication, if they decide to go ahead with it. They will also consider whether they can also promote the writer. Have they plenty of ideas and will they help sales with TV and radio interviews and personal appearances in bookshops? Their view will be strictly commercial so give close consideration to this aspect before approaching them.

TV companies may be approached with plays, series and/or documentaries in similar fashion so you need to be clear about the likely audience and times of day when they are likely to be watching.

Writers earn royalties from publishers who will usually agree an advance payment against future earnings but, with new writers, this is unlikely to be bountiful and provides no guarantee that they will actually publish as they may decide other productions should take priority. It is for these reasons that you need the help of a professional when actually negotiating contracts.

Other forms of writing will appeal to different markets, particularly if you have expertise and/or reputation in a specialist field – travel, hobbies, sport, etc. You could approach magazines in these fields with a couple of articles and a list of headings of planned further articles and secure a contract as a freelance. Similarly you might approach a local newspaper and offer a series on a particular subject that would be of general interest.

Short stories could be offered to magazines with a more general readership and some magazines offer prizes for stories on a theme or situation. Prizes are modest but do give credibility.

The commercial market should not be ignored by those with a special bent. Larger companies might be interested in publishing a monthly newsletter for staff, or professional firms might like a series of client case histories that emphasise a particular feature of their service that brought benefit and could be used as PR.

**Creative writers should also think creatively about markets for their work and skills.**

I find it quite stimulating to walk down the Bayswater Road in London on a Sunday morning once in a while and look at a wide range of creative artistic work that embraces all types of paintings and sculptures in a variety of materials, and designs of costume jewellery, photography and other creations that are being offered for sale by the artists who talk freely about the inspiration for their products and hope to sell enough to enable them to produce more the following week.

Most of these artists probably struggle to make a living, but are dedicated and no doubt exhibit in other locations and hope to make a breakthrough at some point or obtain commissions to produce a work of art from prospective patrons. It is, of course, a desperately competitive business or, more correctly, vocation but, for those involved, they must find a way of communicating with a potential market.

Clearly for those described above, they are using the product itself as a means of communicating, much as a retailer might do, but without the overheads. This has obvious merit but gives the impression of selling a one-off or small collection, with no sense of being aimed at a target market. A seascape is a seascape, but who is going to buy other than on an impulse? My theme is to use your skills to build a commercial enterprise, albeit only a one person business.

This really means you must become known for something – portrait painting, wedding photography, bracelet design, bronze animals, hand-painted pottery and so forth, whereby the nature of the finished product helps define a market sector. A wedding photographer, for instance, might build a small montage of bridal snapshots and use it as a small display that they invite all likely wedding reception venues within their area to display, obviously with contact details as part of the presentation. They could further back this up by contacting all people who announce their engagement in local papers offering to provide the photo album.

A portrait painter might contact all the privately owned companies of any substance in the locality and offer to paint a portrait of the founder to hang in the boardroom. This type of painting could probably be sold for a few thousand pounds to a specific target rather than a few hundred pounds on the Bayswater Road. You could follow through with any successes by offering to paint the founder's spouse.

This type of approach to founders of companies will again need a bought in database of all such companies within the area to whom a creative interest-rouser could be sent or direct approach by telephone. My instinct would be to do both with a gap of about ten days between as there is chance of an immediate response to a creative mail-shot about something less usual.

## Inventors

The UK has a fine reputation for producing great engineers, designers and free thinkers who have created notable inventions, designs and concepts, many of which have achieved world renown. The country has a far worse reputation for bringing these concepts to market and many of our best designs have been launched in other countries. In part I believe this is due to inventors not truly understanding what is involved in creating a market for a product. It is also human nature to fantasise about the value of a product and/ or to fear a loss of control, and yet history shows that great businesses have been built on one invention that has been modified and improved and modernised progressively, but I cannot think of very few businesses that have been created and run by the original inventor. Invention and running commercial undertakings require quite different skills from each other and a wise man understands his limitations.

The key to making money out of an invention is to ensure it finds the right market as quickly as possible and that it is fully exploited by an organisation with sufficient financial muscle to push it as far as it will go. If this is achieved everybody involved will profit. If not, it is highly likely that somebody else will develop something better while you are still arguing over the unrealised spoils.

In Chapter 7 I talked about product specification in relation to defining its place in the market and being clear about the advantages it has over existing products, processes or designs and in this chapter I have talked extensively about defining the features and the benefits they bring in relation to all the other one person businesses under discussion. The inventor's true objectives are to find the person or businesses that recognise the advantages and exploit them accordingly and thereby optimise the inventor's reward emotionally and financially. By following such a strategy you will generate the funds and the time to enable you to concentrate on the next project.

The inventor is, in reality, in the same position as every other person starting a business, in need of a customer(s) and must therefore define their potential outlets and consider how best to approach them. Let us assume a small hand-held suction device that can be flashed across a computer and other office equipment once a week that sucks the dust off the keyboard and screen. It could also be used on paintings and bookcases more efficiently than dusting and polishing. (It may already exist, but I have not seen one.)

At first sight the market is immense, potentially in excess of 25 million in the UK alone, but it is a bit of a gimmick so not everybody will buy one. Made out of plastic with a small motor, switch and changeable dust collection bag it could probably be produced, in bulk, for substantially less than a fiver and might be brought to market for under £10, ideally. If it achieved sales of half a million a year the annual turnover would be £5 million, but who would sell it and how?

The inventor with something new and different has more options than other people in service industries where their markets are defined by what they are – surveyors, barbers, carpenters, IT specialists, etc. You could approach this market through computer manufacturers, slightly unlikely, but if you did persuade one of them to go with it, you would be into a world market. The furniture industry might be interested, or household product manufacturers or mail order companies who specialise in new products, but that would necessitate finding a manufacturer also. A further option would be to find a distribution company who would sub-contract manufacturing. In truth, despite the novelty of the idea, this is not an easy product to launch on the market. The probability is that somebody taking on this product would need to sell it at not less than five times manufacturing cost, but would still want to set an attractive price to the consumer. The product cost would have to be hammered down to circa £1.50 to achieve a retail price of £9.99, inclusive of VAT of £1.67.

Even achieving the first step on the ladder would take a big marketing exercise. You would need to identify in the order of a thousand chief executives of businesses and contact them through a brief letter that stresses the benefits of the invention and describes what it does rather than what it is, indicating the goal of a retail price of less than £10 per unit. This should be followed by a telephone call one week later. You would need to set up 50 top level meetings across the industry sectors who might be interested.

This is quite a tough programme to implement and it could easily take a year and might not succeed. This is the primary reason I stressed working for industry sectors that are constantly seeking new products – novelties, gifts, toys, fashion products, package design. Most industries seek product improvements but usually achieve these by running their own research and design departments. The bottle manufacturing industry, for instance, currently produces bottles of the same tensile strength as those manufactured 50 years ago, but at perhaps only 25 per cent of the former weight and thickness. This is obviously a continuing cost reduction exercise, but also about improving aesthetic design and appearance to marketers and end users.

This is, of course, an ongoing process in most industry sectors. The point at issue, however, is that you must know something about the market you are trying to serve in order to be able to communicate with the principal manufacturers, marketers and distributors who supply the ultimate end users.

# 9 *Pricing your product or service*

It is often said that the market fixes the price and there is a great deal of truth in this statement. It sometimes makes you feel that all businesses operate in cartels but, nevertheless, where this applies, you need to have strong reasons for offering a different price. As indicated in Chapter 4 you can quickly establish what the market price or range of prices is by contacting established practitioners directly or indirectly. Most will give a clear indication about hourly rates but, quite rightly, hesitate to make a commitment to complete within a fixed period before seeing the job. In this respect it should be noted that an estimate is not usually legally binding unless turned into a commitment.

Those who prevaricate too much, however, are often seen as slippery and manipulative. Longer term this can be damaging. Problems are rarely provided for in family budgets so when they occur it is likely to be a financial problem for many customers and they will expect to be told up front how much they need to find and can become extremely irate if the bill comes in for significantly more than the estimate.

Cutting prices is sometimes seen as a way into the market and may be justified in the short term but something I would strongly advise against as an ongoing policy. Price competition must result in lower profitability for all practitioners in the sector and inevitably lead to some closing. If you did your original homework before starting up, you should have established the market had room for your services and that there is no need to cut prices. Nevertheless, pricing is a business tool and, if you are overwhelmed with work, you should consider increasing prices and vice versa.

## Skilled trades

Most single person, skilled tradesmen normally charge an hourly rate, particularly where working on smaller jobs that are unlikely to take longer than a day to complete. For larger jobs, however, customers usually seek a fixed price and may ask several people to quote. This needs handling with care and should always be put in writing, describing what you will do, making clear that any extras to agreed specifications will be charged additionally. It is quite common for customers to ask for something else to be done 'while you are here' or to change their mind about certain features that do cost extra money and this could lead to arguments. It is therefore important to have a clearly defined reference point. Note any amendments the customer asks for and discuss the cost implications, agree an additional price and ask him to sign the agreed variation. This will avoid arguments at a later stage.

There will probably be more hassle in seeking out the bigger jobs, meeting customers, defining precisely what they want and finally writing the specification and pricing the job. The advantage, of course, is that when you do start such a project you do not lose time travelling between jobs and you can add handling charges to any materials you buy, rather than charging out on a purely time basis. The bigger jobs should be more profitable depending on how intense the competition is.

The second factor in pricing work is ensuring you are paid. With smaller jobs you should seek to be paid immediately. Carry an invoice pad with duplicate copy and write it out by hand. If the customer says they cannot pay you now, ask when you might be able to collect cash or a cheque when nearby and make sure you call. In other cases, state 'Cash within 14 days'. A one person business is, in effect, working for wages, and cannot afford to give credit or risk bad debts. If money due isn't paid within 14 days, call the customer on the telephone during the evening and pin them down to immediate payment. Keep records and dates of such calls and ring again if the customer does not meet the commitment.

### Terms of trade

With experience you will learn to be up front about
money matters. When taking the call tell the customer
when you expect to arrive and ask that they let you
have cash or a cheque when the work is completed.
You may be asked for a price so give an hourly rate,
advising that you do not know how long it will take
without seeing the problem, but indicate 'in the order
of, depending . . .'

If you are intending to focus on larger jobs, such as
household re-wiring, fitted kitchens, central heating
installations, house painting, garden re-design, it
will pay you to ask a solicitor to write out briefly the
terms of trade and have them printed as a leaflet that
you attach to quotations. This should obviously cover
payment terms and should include a substantial deposit.
The amount of deposit will vary according to the nature
of the trade. If it is your responsibility to purchase all
the kitchen fitments, the deposit could be the full cost
of such items plus a mark-up; the same with boilers and
radiators. Where, however, you are merely buying tins
of paint you will probably have to restrict deposits to
25–30 per cent.

### Disputes

Disputes will inevitably arise and should be anticipated
within your specified terms of trade, agreeing to rectify
wherever the work carried out does not conform to the
agreed specification or where something is obviously
faulty, but ensure your liability is limited to such things
and try not to be caught on timetables. If, for instance,

the customer demands it must be fitted by the end of
May and you know this timetable is tight, add a bonus
to the price and negotiate to limit penalties for late
completion.

Be warned, however, that this is often a genuine
grievance for many customers where work is started
and then nobody appears for a couple of weeks and
the family continues to live among the rubble. Such
situations can be infuriating for many customers,
particularly where structural work is being carried
out or fitments replaced. Try to avoid such situations
as a matter of policy as complaints of this nature are
damaging to reputations.

Notwithstanding that remedial work will be necessary
from time to time, there are customers who will pick
fault as a matter of course and seek to secure discounts
for what they may describe as shoddy work or try to
suggest some things are not up to expectations. It is
at times like this that you need to be able to refer to
specifications and quotations. Be polite, but firm.

As a general rule try to avoid litigation but do not
be afraid to use it, particularly for smaller sums that
can be brought in the Small Claims Court. If your
documentation is satisfactory you can handle this type
of claim without a solicitor. The Court will usually
bend in favour of somebody who has set out clearly
what he intends to do and is able to demonstrate that
such work has been carried out. The defendant is
immediately placed in a difficult position and trying to
justify complaints without any evidence.

### Insurances

Insurance cover is a virtual necessity for tradesmen who might cause damage to passers by, i.e. spill paint all over them or they might trip over tools and accessories. Tradesmen are also vulnerable. They could fall off ladders, electrocute themselves or cause damage to property and so need comprehensive cover for all these potential disasters. This is easily arranged by contacting a local insurance broker who will advise you about your needs and arrange cover. Brokers earn commission on the products they sell so do discuss these issues carefully and do not take unnecessary protective cover. I will deal with Life Assurance and pensions later on.

## Personal services

The market price is usually easy to obtain for businesses that generally operate from High Street premises as they are normally displayed within. They are less obvious for music teachers, reflexologists, tutors, fitness counsellors, etc., so research will be necessary. Calls can be made to competitors to enquire and most will tell you immediately, generally assuming you are a potential client.

For those services provided from retail-type premises it is implicit that payment is immediately required before leaving so it is almost essential to have a credit card facility. People in these occupations usually carry a small stock of products used in the service – hair conditioners, make-up, fragrances and balms, which help add to income and are readily saleable with only a tiny effort. For other services, while immediate payment is not implicit, it is good practice to demand payment at the end of each session as the treatments or lessons usually cost less than £100 per time, hence reasonably affordable, and again a credit card facility is desirable. There is a danger in granting credit, particularly if providing weekly or monthly sessions, whereby the service can begin to look expensive if left for two or three months and, in reality, credit should not be necessary for these types of services.

Terms of trade are more obvious in personal services so do not need to be carefully defined. Disputes of any consequence are also uncommon as the most likely downside is to refund the charge. Accidents can and do happen so some professional indemnity insurance should be taken out to cover mishaps.

## Professional services

Lawyers, accountants and independent doctors usually charge an hourly rate which might vary according to the type of work they are doing, i.e. tax advice will probably be charged at a higher rate than bookkeeping services. Architects and surveyors often take a percentage of the project or charge hourly rates if percentages are not appropriate. Clients increasingly prefer a fixed rate for the job, but lawyers in particular have difficulty accepting this as developments in most cases are almost impossible to predict. Complications do arise and, quite often, the client has not provided all the facts or been less than candid about how a dispute arose so it is difficult to quote an overall price.

Many lawyers are particularly cautious about this, sometimes to the point of evasion that, again, may work against their longer-term interest and can be irksome when they claim to have recovered £1,000 from the defendant and submit a fee invoice for £2,000. This is demonstrably poor value for the client, but not confined to lawyers. Repairs to a product that could be replaced for less than the cost of repairs are equally damaging. You will never hear from that client/customer again and they are certain to bad mouth you. Providing a demonstrably poor value service can also be viewed as something of a scam.

Other factors do arise with professional practices in that one of the objectives, in many cases, is to develop a client base of people who will generate repeat business. This is particularly true of accountants who produce annual accounts, tax returns and audits that recur from year to year, but also true for architects and surveyors working with developers and builders who seek new projects from time to time. Many surveyors are listed with building societies to carry out property valuations and this, too, is constantly repeating business. Many of these relationships continue for more than a decade.

Teachers also work with children, coaching them over a period of time. Most families have more than one child so, again, teachers should be looking to work with families for perhaps five years. Chiropractors and osteopaths are frequently dealing with back problems that for many patients never quite go away so repeat business is part of their practice growth strategy.

Doctors and lawyers deal with specific problems that usually occur suddenly so their interest is more about satisfying clients so that they obtain referrals.

The reality of all professional businesses, however, is that they are selling time, usually at attractive rates, but time is a limiting factor on how far the business is able to expand and also a pressure to ensure that time is not wasted.

## Management services

A daily rate (or per diem) is the norm with consultancy-type services but packages are often more attractive to both parties, particularly where part of the package is almost stereotyped and held on computer. Part can be tailored for specific clients but the main section remains virtually constant.

In earlier chapters we talked about creating a database and approaching prospective clients directly. You may also find a variety of recruitment agencies in many fields who provide interim and/or temporary managers or specialists to customers. It would be worthwhile talking to such agents and indeed seeking work through them initially to help gain experience of working as a solo practitioner. The going rate for ex-middle managers who are qualified engineers, accountants, surveyors, etc., is in the order of only £200/250 per day in the home counties and probably less as you go further out of London. An interim finance director, however, might well earn close to £100,000 for a nine-month stint.

In dealing direct with commercial clients the price will depend to a large extent on how you are perceived and what they feel you can bring to the party. The clue here is to define a project you can work on and assess its value to the company wherever possible. As an IT specialist you might agree to implement a system that combines order taking, with delivery instructions to the warehouse and produces invoices simultaneously, thereby effecting staff savings of £100,000 p.a. once installed. You might calculate that it will take three months to carry out the assignment and negotiate on the basis of a share of the first year savings.

In the above example you have a specific goal and a basis for negotiating an attractive rate but this would be less true if you are offering a marketing campaign that is likely to cost the company £100,000 to implement. Here you might agree a three-week assignment to make an in-depth study at a fixed cost followed by a retainer of one day per week to oversee the introduction of the scheme. This type of package can be attractive to clients by making them feel they do not need full-time employees and you could thereby command a higher rate of £500/600 per day with the right to re-negotiate one year later if the campaign was demonstrably successful. There is a great advantage to the solo consultant of having a few retainers and ongoing, part-time work. Accountants, HR managers and systems analysts, etc., can offer similar packages and with small- to medium-sized companies establish themselves as an essential part-time member of the management team.

You may have to balance the duration of the project against your daily rate. If a company is offering you three days work a week you might handle this at £250 per day compared to a normal daily rate of £400, for instance. This could be to your long-term advantage, however, as you have no further marketing expense or activity to set against it and, if the project proves valuable to your client, you could negotiate higher rates as time goes by, or perhaps agree to cut to two days per week for possibly £650.

It is usually a face-to-face negotiation and, when starting out, you are in a weak position, but it pays to be bullish, provided you do not make yourself sound too expensive. Remember also that you have to work with other members of the team. If the works director is only earning £35,000 p.a. he will look askance at you earning £45,000 for a three-day week although you can point out you buy and run your own car, the company bears no National Insurance cost and your holidays are unpaid leave.

In some cases pricing is a complicated part of the mix. For instance, a specialist in stocks and shares might decide to embark on a lecture tour to promote a system that provides buying and selling signals. The expert would be faced with upfront costs – rent of a conference centre, hire of temporary staff, provision of catering services, promoting the event. This might well amount to £10,000, so at £500 per head it would need to attract a minimum of 20 respondents to break even. The centre or hotel might only take a maximum of

50 attendees so, on the upside, a one-day presentation could make £15,000 profit but you cannot be sure how many people are willing to attend and pay £500. There may be a trade off between price and numbers that would be very hard to judge without experience of staging similar events so you face a tricky decision – a trade off between price and volume. There is often a close inter-relationship that is not easy to judge unless you can bring a clincher, i.e. a reputation as a financial journalist, references from people who have successfully used the system and so on. Well-known successful speakers in this field can command £1,000 per ticket and fill an auditorium of 100 people. It would, however, be difficult to envisage a speaker on model railways attracting such an audience

## General trading, internet and mail order

Again, in many cases, a market price will be available, particularly where you are selling competitive products. Most people know how much they pay for a shirt or tennis racket and, if tempted to buy through mail order or the internet, they are usually looking for bargains. Hence many companies, selling consumable products, constantly promote: 'Three shirts for the price of two' or 'Final reductions on last year's stock'.

Where price is not known you should make detailed comparisons of your product against similar products and evaluate the differences. For instance, somebody might be selling a paint that needs two coats to achieve an attractive finish whereas your paint only needs one. If competition charges £8.99 per litre, you could reasonably justify a price in excess of £15 per litre, all other things being equal, but your advertising would need to explain the price difference and stress the advantages.

In this section we are talking about one person businesses with limited funds; let us say a maximum of £10,000 to spend on products. This is immediately a limiting factor, and a critical consideration therefore is the length of time needed to complete the business cycle to determine how frequently you can turn over your money.

For instance, you might import a consignment of 1,000 widgets from Poland that you buy at £10 each and can sell at £15 each. Initially this looks like a 50 per cent profit, but the actual calculation is:

| | |
|---|---|
| Selling price – £15×1,000 items | 15,000 |
| Less VAT included in price | 2,234 |
| Net sales value | 12,766 |
| Purchase price | 10,000 |
| Net profit<br>27.66% | 2,766 |

This may be a satisfactory return if you are able to do the transaction once per week but, if you have a delivery time from your supplier to warehouse of a week before you promote and orders build up over three weeks and dribble in thereafter you have a minimum four weeks cycle before you can place your next order, hence you can promote only a dozen times per year. Theoretically this would produce a profit of circa £35,000 p.a., but you are almost certain to have returns, unlikely to be less than two per cent, frequently more and you may not sell your entire stock. Indeed, if you are selling a range of sizes you will have to guess how many of each size before placing your purchase order and such a guess will almost certainly be wrong, but you can try to get the balance right with future purchases. Even so, you will be left with some stock that you have to sell off at lower prices and you will have to carry out promotions intermittently, meaning further discounts, to generate sales. The above calculation also ignores advertising and promotion or other costs of selling.

With limited capital it is, however, a business that could be started from home before quitting the day job. Most direct response businesses utilise the services of a fulfilment house so place an order with a supplier who delivers to the fulfilment house who acts as stockist. Respondents call or write to the fulfilment house that also arranges delivery and accepts cheques or credit card payments on your behalf. They transfer all cash received, usually weekly, together with a list of orders from customers with their details, enabling you to build a database of customers.

Having placed the initial order and produced copy and placed advertisements, you have little to do except monitor progress until you place the next orders and adverts. This would give you the opportunity to build capital and customer base, as well as learning some of the pitfalls before relying on the income for the first six to twelve months, and to assess the risks accordingly.

Typically, mail order companies sell products at five times the purchase cost. This allows them to cover advertising and postage costs. In many cases they also place contingent orders with suppliers whereby they supply the fulfilment house with products but must accept returns if the merchandise doesn't sell. Not everything does sell.

Internet selling can work on smaller margins as they do not bear mailing costs and usually advertise at far lower cost, particularly if referring potential respondents to their website.

## Agents

The price is usually fixed by the principal but much will depend on the type of product you are dealing with and on the nature of the agreement. Where the arrangement is strictly commission on sales with the customer paying the principal direct, you have no scope to vary prices. If, however, you are required to hold demonstration models and buy direct from the principal, you are in a negotiating position. There is unlikely to be scope for reducing the purchase price but it is sometimes possible, particularly with larger orders, say three or four machines. You are not bound by a recommended price to the customer and could therefore lower or raise the final price, depending on circumstances, competitive pressures or lack of, etc.

For the most part an agent is dealing with fixed or known prices with little opportunity to adjust.

## Creative people

The most common arrangement is to secure royalties from the company to whom you effectively assign the rights to your creation and to hope they will achieve predicted sales. There are variations on this theme whereby authors secure an advance of royalties, frequently as high as the amount they are expected to earn out of the deal. Certain rights could be excluded, i.e. film rights or foreign sales or character merchandising opportunities so that additional income can be obtained from other sources, but with any literary work that is likely to achieve high sales, you are strongly advised to use a professional agent. It is a potential minefield.

Articles for newspapers are normally outright sales, but again need handling with care. Be sure to point out that you are seeking payment and not simply contributing your view to the newspaper, and make clear that copyright will revert to you after a period of time. You may be able to use it again in different fashion a few years downstream.

Film-scripts and plays need backers so are often outright sales, but again for a limited period only. This

type of deal can be in stages, i.e. you might earn a
nominal amount for a play that opens in the provinces
with a further stage payment if it runs in the West End
and more if it runs beyond a certain length of time.
Be sure to retain some hold over copyright in all these
circumstances. Successful plays could be staged all over
the world and, if so, you want to earn from each event.

Artists are in a different position to writers in that
customers usually take exclusive possession of the
finished product. It is rare to have a known market
price before a painting or sculpture is sold so nobody
knows the true worth. Artists do, however, create a
reputation and the more widely known they become,
the higher the price of their work. This often requires
the support of patrons or experts who are willing to
stage exhibitions in galleries and invite known collectors
to special viewings. This, however, is more for the
fortunate few with considerable talent, but does give an
indication of how to market oneself, even if only in local
towns like Bath or Chester.

Displaying a collection in a local gallery is likely to
generate more sales, particularly if you are able to
attract some press coverage and local promotion. In
many such cases you are using the gallery owner as
a commission agent who may set an asking price or
suggest 'offers above a certain figure'.

In an earlier chapter I indicated that portrait painters
could approach company chairman and perhaps quote
figures in the order of £3,000, raising prices quite
rapidly if they find a ready market.

Specialist photographers should be able to assess the market price in their local area quite readily and promote themselves accordingly. Many general photographers tend to open retail units where most of their income is derived from developing customers' photographs and the sale of cameras and frames, etc. Freelance photographers are in a highly speculative business where they are hoping to capture a moment or incident but, realistically, this needs combining with other activities to be sure of making a living.

Inventors typically earn a five per cent rental but such royalty is still negotiable and deals can be structured to provide a higher figure above a certain level of sales. Care has to be taken to define what is meant by price. In many industries the royalty relates to a retail price, in others the manufactured price. In the latter case the inventor should seek higher royalties.

Where a significant invention is being sought by more than one potential distributor, negotiations can be extended to cover not only higher royalties but also down payments in advance and a minimum annual royalty. For an inventor working within a specific industry where a reputation has been established, advance royalties can usually be secured.

Designers are often in a different position. A package designer working in the cosmetics industry, for instance, will probably go for an outright sale of the design which is usually bespoke for a particular product and is only a part of the product's overall cost. The cost of producing the actual package may not be known until the cosmetic company starts producing and the packaging producer is unlikely to have any commercial relationship with the designer and probably no certainty of continuity of supplying the cosmetic company.

In most areas of creativity there is no known price or certain value so it will usually be to the creator's advantage to engage a professional negotiator to assist, somebody who knows and understands the market. Even net of their commissions they will usually generate a higher net income than the creator is likely to achieve single-handed.

# 10 *Calculating risk and breakeven*

There is inevitably risk in business as indeed there is in life itself. I have always smiled at the expression that: 'If you want to make God laugh, tell him your plans'. Even so, planning is an essential business tool but, for a new starter in business, it is difficult to quantify in financial terms. The range of probability is quite large. When you have been in business for a few years it becomes much easier to predict your income and, if you have been reasonably successful, the limiting factor could well be how much time you have available.

I remember when I first launched out on my own and met my first prospect who arranged to meet me the following day. I did a couple of hours' preparatory work, but the guy didn't show up. I was bitterly disappointed, but two years later, when another client failed to appear, I merely shrugged my shoulders and carried on with the next thing. When starting out, any changed circumstance is significant, but far less so when you have several clients.

Prediction is almost impossible. The range of probability is extremely wide. In my own case I evolved a technique of working from the downside and trying not to be too clever. The first and paramount objective is to cover your living costs and it may be that you cannot achieve this target for a few months and have to fall back on savings or borrowings. You are confronted with a blank sheet of paper and the 'what if' questions.

## What to do if you do not get an order for six months

This is highly unlikely in most situations but it does bring home the reality of self-employment. You still have to pay the rent or mortgage, the HP on the car and put food on the table. As a single person you can squeeze these costs to the minimum, but less easy if you have a family. Even living on your own costs money and it's hard to contemplate living on much less than £1,000 per month if you have any lifestyle. Costs quickly escalate if you have children. Calculate how much you need merely to live for the first six months. Let's assume £7,500 is the average figure so we have an immediate objective to earn not less than £7,500 in the next six months and to establish a monthly income thereafter of in excess of £1,250. Even this meagre figure ignores tax liability which even for a self-employed person runs at almost £2,000 per annum on an income of £15,000.

## Trade services to the public

Let us assume an average hourly rate of £40 for a tradesman. It will vary according to location and craft but the principle is not affected. You can substitute actual rates earned and re-calculate accordingly. Let us also assume that you have access to a maximum of £5,000, which will disappear quite quickly if you do not start work. Let us further assume that you have to purchase tools to a value of £250 and that for each job you do you need an average of £10 for materials and that the average job takes four hours, including travel time.

We can now calculate:

| | |
|---|---|
| Value of job: 4 hours×£40 | 160 |
| Less materials | 10 |
| Net value | 150 per job |
| Income required | 1,250 |
| Plus tools purchased | 250 |
| | 1,500 |

Number of jobs required to breakeven £1,500 divided by £150

You need only ten jobs per month to cover living costs and pay for tools, but in the second month you do not need to buy tools again so eight jobs will cover personal expenses.

As stated you can substitute figures, i.e. £30 per job lasting three hours less £5 for materials is £85, so you need 18 jobs in the first month and only 15 per month thereafter.

The point about this technique is that it enables you to set simple targets in terms you are able to understand, i.e. if you can secure two four-hour jobs a week or three jobs of three hours each, you do not have to worry about the rent being paid. It is far easier to count to four or five jobs per week and a much easier target to work towards. In my experience it is highly improbable that a start up business would be able to produce cash flow projections for the first year that are even reasonably accurate unless you have long-term contracts to begin with.

Strictly speaking you should add tax, and many self-employed people transfer money monthly to a deposit account to be sure they can meet the liability when it falls due. In the short term, however, you can ignore this and concentrate on the more critical issue of covering your living expenses.

The advantage of using this method rather than financial budgeting and monitoring is that you can handle it mentally. You can quickly assess whether you have done six hours' work in any given week and keep a simple record of how many hours you have worked each week. This is not to say that you should not keep formal accounting records; you should. You need to invoice customers, you need to ensure they pay you, but by keeping a simple goal in mind you can focus on a clear objective without distraction.

There are, of course, many variables between the different occupations but this basic calculation can be used in virtually all one person service businesses. It has the added feature that once you are trading ahead of the breakeven you already have a sense of achievement and can start to feel truly positive about your business prospects.

## Personal services

The yardsticks are precisely the same for those who provide a personal service, but jobs tend to be of shorter duration and the amounts lower and, in some cases like beauty treatments and hairdressing, your cost of materials is likely to be higher, possibly even more than ten per cent of the total charge, but these probably form part of an initial stock you must buy in order to commence business, say £300–400 of cosmetics, replaced periodically, according to progress. You may also be obliged to incur some capital expenditure (more durable assets that wear out over a longer period such as desks, computers, adjustable beds or even pianos). This is obviously a cost you would want to recoup but not with quite the same degree of urgency needed to cover living costs.

As before the calculation is similar:

| | | |
|---|---|---|
| Value of job | say | 50 |
| Less materials | | 10 |
| Net value | | 40 |

Number of jobs needed to cover £7,500 plus materials of £500+

£8,000 divided by 40+200 jobs or 8 per week.

This is again an easy target to keep in mind and, once established, you would probably expect to handle that volume of business daily, but by then it may be necessary to move to commercial premises, increasing your cost base. Even then, you should assess the increased costs, add them to lifestyle costs, calculate an average weekly figure and assess the number of jobs needed. At this stage, however, you should be added a further minimum of 35 per cent to cover tax and National Insurance liabilities, another subject we will cover later. The fundamental point, however, is that you should keep simple targets in mind in order to be constantly aware of how the business is progressing, long before your accountant tells you.

## Professional services

The principles are the same as above but the variables are greater. Most professionals will have some standard products. A surveyor may agree that a valuation of a house on behalf of a building society is a standard fee

or an accountant will probably have a standard fee
for producing a sole trader's annual accounts and tax
return. A solicitor probably knows how much time they
will spend on the conveyance of a house, but will have
little or no idea of how long it might take to resolve
residence issues of a divorcing couple with children,
particularly if they appear to be at loggerheads. In
that many professionals charge an hourly rate, they
can use a standard hour, rather than job rate to do the
calculation set out in the above sections for tradesmen
and providers of a personal service. This will prove to
be broadly acceptable over a longer period of time but
few professionals are in a cash business and therefore
inevitably allow credit and, in many cases, must wait
until a project has been completed before submitting
their invoices. Many lawyers, in particular, tackle
this problem by asking for upfront fees on account.
Accountants engaged on audits for operating companies
find it more difficult to follow this practice and often
have several months of work-in-progress unpaid for at
any one time. Architects, who can be involved with
projects lasting beyond a year, usually apply stage
payments, but this too grants a period of credit which
has to be absorbed.

The majority of people setting up professional practices
have to buy some equipment and furniture and, at the
very least, turn one room of their homes into offices.
This often runs to a few thousand pounds. Even on
a shoestring it is unlikely to be less than a couple of
thousand.

These various factors, taken together, necessitate setting up a forward budgeting and cash spend planning system and, of course, a simple accounting system whereby they can monitor fees billed, income received, and maintain control over outstanding debts to ensure statements are sent out regularly and that debtors are chased. The system needed becomes more complicated for solicitors who hold clients' money.

I will not set out the mechanics of such an accounting system as part of this book, merely recommend that those of you in this situation should engage the services of a competent accountant.

## Management services to industry

Those of you who operate in this type of consultancy capacity are in a position half way between tradesmen and professionals. Most of you do not need a fully furnished office although, in many cases, high quality reports must be produced, but usually you should get by with a computer, printer, mobile and car and some sort of database of potential clients. I have already advocated quite strongly that where you are able to package a service as a product you should do so. It is so much easier to talk about and implies you are in and out within a reasonable amount of time and leave something tangible for the client to use thereafter. Where you are doing this, for the smaller business sector, I recommend a price range of between £1,000–5,000. Once installed, you can always talk about supporting, monitoring or further training roles thereafter, by which time you have given value and proved to be of some benefit to your client. Unless you have something unusual to offer, I think it unlikely you will break into larger corporations with this technique.

With this type of product service you can quickly determine how many services you need to carry out to break even over a short-term period. In other cases you are on a per diem rate and only need to assess how many days you need to work at your given rate to break even.

In any project with clients you should discuss rates of fees and payment terms at the outset. If you are engaged on a longer-term project, try to ensure monthly payments immediately following the month you have worked, i.e. seven days from date of invoice and try to enforce 14-day terms for giving a product service. As a solo consultant you want to be treated as part of the team and paid as quickly as the team members are.

## Internet trading, mail order, etc.

Even though you are not selling time you should start from the same basic calculation and calculate your monthly living costs over the first six months. **Six months is a good timescale in which to establish viability – your second objective.**

As a trader you are, of course, looking to make profits on transactions so this is the criterion, rather than time, but you also have other 'what if' questions like: What if

I don't sell all the stock I have bought? Can I dump it at a lower margin? Will I have to take a loss on it?

Let us be positive. It is implicit that, if you are trading, you do have some cash available, albeit a limited budget. We did, however, argue that it is difficult to start a trading business without some cash and that it is best done as a part-time business until you have adequate resources to generate sufficient sales and margins to provide an income large enough to sustain a living and continue business expansion.

With this type of business you are not providing credit but you may find difficulties in trying to obtain credit, particularly when you first start and almost certainly if importing. So we have to assume you must pay for product upfront but there is nothing to stop you promoting the products before you receive delivery, and you should take cash before you deliver to your customers. The nature of this type of promotion, however, is that business rolls in over a period of time, particularly when using the internet. The more expensive the product the longer customers will take to make their minds up to buy. Inevitably there will be returns for a variety of reasons including damaged goods which are probably of no further use to you.

Circumstances will vary according to the type of products being sold. If you are selling a range of sizes it will, of course, be difficult to predict with any precision how much stock to hold of each size but if you stick to the same product range throughout the year, topping up stocks as they become depleted, you will eventually be able to maintain closer control over this. Shirt companies have become particularly successful in the mail order business, so much so that most of them now offer a complete range of menswear and even add some products for women. With these types of product, however, you are ultimately offering a wide range of choice, in colours, styles and sizes that are far beyond the scope of a one person business who is better advised to look for specialist-type products with very high margins. Ideally one seeks a low cost product that could be sold for many times its production cost, hence information publishing has attracted a large number of entrants into the marketplace, particularly in the get rich quick areas like forex trading, dealing in stocks and shares, etc.

Even in these markets it is a slow build because the objectives are somewhat different to service companies. To succeed it is vital to build a mailing list of people who buy the products you sell with the longer-term goal of trying to ensure a higher response rate from mailing lists. Let us take a simple case of a product that costs £5 which you import without paying VAT but sell at £30 inclusive of £5 VAT. You rent out a mail list of 10,000 names at 15 pence per name, prepare sales literature, buy and stuff envelopes and post. With the recent rise in the cost of postage it is likely to cost £1 per mail-shot for delivery. You are committed to the following expenses:

| | |
|---|---|
| Rent of mail list | 1,500 |
| Mail-shots | 10,000 |
| | 11,500 |

You make a net profit of £20 per product sold. You therefore need to sell 575 products to break even, a response rate of 5.75 per cent. This would actually be a very high response rate to a cold promotion of a single product which, of course, is one of the reasons why mail order companies develop a range or offer a catalogue of products with the concept that if you don't sell one product sell something else. The probability is that you will make a loss on your early mailings until you have acquired a list of names of people who have bought from you and are willing to do so again. Ideally the second time, they will buy more expensive products with better margins.

The cost of promoting over the internet is significantly less than mail order but the response rate is dramatically lower, hence you need time to build this type of business which is why I recommend starting slowly while you still have other income and build your mailing list slowly. If you can achieve a situation where you have 2,000–3,000 customers who buy something from you every year you will ultimately have a good business.

## Agents

An agent is in a similar position to a provider of services whereby you should assess how many widgets to sell to cover the first six months' budget, based on the commission earned per widget. This is reasonably straightforward although with the more expensive items – capital equipment in particular – it is likely to take longer to negotiate initial orders, but the arithmetic is the same.

Some complexity may arise if you are required to hold stock or demonstration machines, in which case you are seeking to recover these costs as well as cover living expenses.

## Creative occupations

People following these vocations are not initially operating in the business world at all until they have created something and, as described in previous sections, they are possibly only seeking one customer thereafter to launch their creations unless choosing to take an initial business approach of finding a customer first and creating the work that they want.

A freelance journalist would be in a similar situation to a sales agent, for instance, whereby they could reasonably calculate the number of articles they need to write to cover living expenses. An author might take a commission to write a travel book for a publishing company, in which case they should negotiate an advance and a designer might secure a similar contract from a commercial enterprise. In such cases they are using creative talent under guidance about what the end product has to achieve, and the budgetary and break-even considerations are the same as for other professions described above.

There is no logical way, however, of predicting how and when a new creative concept will reach a point at which it can be credibly considered or when it will bear fruit in commercial terms.

# 11 *Using other services and professionals*

You cannot know how to do everything or solve every problem yourself and it is foolish to try. There is usually a great deal more skill required to being a tradesman or professional than appears on the surface and, even if you can make a reasonable fist of some other occupations, it is certain to take you much longer to complete the task. It is often tempting to believe you can save money by carrying out extraneous functions yourself, but usually misguided.

I suggested early in this discourse that many one person businesses are perceived as problem solvers and they are often as valuable to other business operators as they are to homeowners or other individuals. It is better to hire these skills on an as wanted basis rather than engaging specialist staff yourself. There are many hidden costs with full-time staff. You have to find work for them. This is sometimes harder than finding work for yourself and, if unable to find sufficient work for staff, you are paying for idle time as well as their holidays and sickness bouts.

Profits are taxed and VAT is imposed the moment your business does £77,000 turnover in any 12-month period so many businesses find it helpful to appoint an accountant. This is likely to be a long-term relationship so choose with care. You want somebody to whom you can talk and who is available on the telephone or responds quickly to emails and who is essentially on your side. This last point is important. There are legal tax breaks and your business can be structured to minimise tax. You need to be advised of these things.

You need to produce annual accounts and have them agreed with the Inland Revenue. This is a service most accountants offer, usually for a few hundred pounds per annum for the single person business. They know what expenses can be set against income and what can't and so they are able to determine and agree tax liabilities with the Inland Revenue without much hassle. In this respect, however, it must be said that from around the turn of the last century the Inland Revenue have become much more aggressive and have clearly been under government pressure to raise as much money as possible. This has led to a much higher incidence of queries and investigations than in any earlier decade. However, if your accountant has guided you sensibly, this should be readily defended. Virtually every business needs an accountant within a year of starting up, if not sooner.

Most other professionals you should only engage on an as needed basis, although if you are in the property business it is as well to work with specialist lawyers, surveyors and architects. Most small businesses, however, should only need professional help on an occasional basis. After consultation with other professionals you should be careful to define, in writing, what service you want. Architects and surveyors usually need a fairly precise brief. Lawyers like to quote an hourly rate and leave the matter open. This is often necessary, but solicitors are charging typically in the order of £200 per hour, and significantly more in London, so you need to understand what they are going to do and be clear about what they should not do.

Solicitors frequently begin their letters with: 'We are instructed by . . .' In your own interests make sure you instruct them carefully and as precisely as possible. Confirm in writing, particularly where potential problems might arise, and review at intervals to be confident that matters are proceeding the way you want. I stress this particular aspect because it is an area where you are quickly spending money in thousands of pounds which might not turn out to be money well spent, especially if your emotions are involved.

Insurances too should be taken out at an early stage so some contact with a broker is desirable. They usually earn commissions, paid by the insurance companies with whom they place the business.

## Tradesmen

There should be little call for professional advice in the early stages of your business. You probably should engage an accountant immediately, particularly if you have no knowledge or experience of raising invoices and keeping records, but here again, proceed with caution. You almost certainly do not need computerised systems that you do not fully understand, and most accountants should be able to produce annual accounts from basic records and bank account statements.

It is also worthwhile to have a commercial solicitor draw up 'terms of trade' that you should have printed as a leaflet, for inclusion with quotations and on the back of your invoices. Thereafter you should be able to tick along without further assistance.

Many tradesmen do become involved in part of a customer's total scheme whereby they are fitting a new up-to-date kitchen with all the latest gadgetry, for instance. The majority of such customers will want somebody to coordinate the entire project. In most cases, probably the kitchen supplier as many firms offer package deals, but not always. In just imagining what goes on it is obvious that the customer will need a basic fitter/joiner, a plumber, an electrician and a painter. Most customers will want the work to be carried out simultaneously, where possible, and sequentially without unnecessary delays as they will be without a kitchen while work is in progress.

If, for instance, you are a kitchen fitter it would be reasonable to be able to fit new taps over a sink, or connect a cooker to the electricity supply. It would be unrealistic, however, for most fitters to move sinks, install dishwashers and washing machines, bring water supplies to them and connect to outlets and drains as well as fit housing units and cabinets. There are many tradesmen who can do all of these jobs, but, if charged with carrying out the full kitchen installation and pricing it accordingly you should think in terms of bringing in a plumber and an electrician who could be on site at the same time as you. The whole project will come together faster and more efficiently from the customer's viewpoint with a high probability that it will be finished to professional standards.

This situation could be approached in one of two ways. You could elect to be a sub-contractor and make yourself known to all kitchen installers in your neighbourhood or you could undertake to manage the job and pull a team together. As overall coordinator you would inevitably be involved in carrying out more work, pricing the project, planning the installation, ensuring the right skills are available at the right time and, indeed, that all the necessary fitments are ordered with delivery dates clearly agreed. You would obviously expect to be rewarded for this extra work and so must build your time into the quotation and a mark-up on the equipment, fitments and sub-contractors.

A project of this nature brings us full circle to where we started by suggesting you must determine the market you want to serve. Most will be content to stick to their core skills, but the more ambitious will be tempted to follow this route with its attendant stresses. When managing projects of this nature, contingencies should be built into the price and the contracts carefully negotiated with both customers and sub-contractors. Fixed rates are preferable as a piece of equipment might not turn up or unanticipated problems with plumbing or wiring might emerge and you do not want skilled tradesmen standing around waiting for the problems to be solved.

## Personal services

As above, accountants will be needed on the same terms and conditions and insurance risks covered. With many personal services that start from a room in your home there is an interim objective to move to premises where you are visible to passers-by or where you want to equip salons or consulting rooms. At this point you need to take care in negotiating the terms of the rental. Throughout most of the second half of the last century landlords in many parts of the country felt able to impose their own terms which could be sometimes onerous, including clauses like complete re-decoration of premises and renovation of fixtures and fittings on surrender of the lease for whatever reason. They also asked for periodic rent reviews, upwards only.

I have usually felt the terms to be one-sided, but I do believe times are changing. Retail businesses are no longer as profitable as they used to be as more people are buying, even basic requirements, on the internet and through catalogues. Recession in the last few years has driven many retailers out of business. Shops are available in towns up and down the country and deals can be done. Even so, leases are complex and it pays to employ a solicitor to guide you through the detail and possibly re-negotiate any clauses that might still be too tough on the tenant.

Another possibility worth consideration is a growing trend towards one stop service centres. As a consequence supermarkets are increasingly selling a much wider range of goods and even supplying services such as insurances and edging their way into banking. This is happening too with professional services, particularly with international accountants and lawyers who are into offering both services and also property valuations, acquisitions and disposals and complete packages relating to mergers and takeovers of businesses. In a smaller way this is happening with centres where women, in particular, may have a manicure while their hair is being styled, followed by beauty treatments and make-up. Such services are increasingly being offered to brides, their mothers and bridesmaids at the bride's home as a premium service.

This, in many ways, is similar to the package deals offered by tradesmen, as described above. One of the group of service providers probably holds the head lease and sub-lets rooms to the others and coordinates the total service. In other cases, luxury hotels offer a range of therapies and treatments on site through concessions or franchise arrangements. The package service is again usually more profitable for the person handling coordination of treatments. As always, it is wealthier clients who demand the comprehensive packages so prices are generally higher.

## Professional services

The legal and medical professions are among the earliest types of businesses formed and have been available in one form or other throughout known history. As such they have become a virtual part of the establishment. The Judiciary most certainly is, but the Law Society and British Medical Council also carry a heavy clout.

Other professions have equally become self-regulating and have gained royal charters and the prestige that goes with them, hence they are reasonably close knit and kept well informed of legal, business and social developments by their professional bodies. They are well educated and generally aware and well able to provide services and advice to clients. As a consequence, they have access and entry into clubs and associations and so automatically network with other professionals, develop good contacts and recommend clients to each other in a mutually supportive way.

Clearly for any professional setting up in business for the first time it must pay to edge his or her way into these clubs, associations and networks, many of which are also highly supportive of charities in their local communities.

## Management services

Solo consultants should also seek to gain entry into the type of associations that professional people use as they too provide high level, specialist advice and you could benefit from networking in similar fashion. The nature of their work, however, is with companies who already employ managers within the business and only resort to outside services when seeking special skills. The directors would probably be willing to interview people recommended by consultants but will ultimately choose the people they want working inside their organisation. There are, of course, some exceptions. A specialist in marketing may sub-contract some work to copywriters, for instance, when preparing advertising materials and literature for their client or an accountant may recommend specific software, but most of the time consultants will be working on their own initiative.

## Selling via the internet, mail order, etc.

It is usual in this type of business to sub-contract most supporting services. The major activity is the holding of stock, acceptance of orders and payments and arranging delivery. There are several fulfilment houses up and down the country who provide this service for quite modest charges. Most sales over the internet or through mail order catalogues charge postage and packing as an extra and this is usually sufficient to cover the fulfilment service charges. For anybody launching direct response type businesses this is an essential back-up service that I strongly recommend.

As with all things it pays to look around as both the nature and price vary, so you should visit to see what they do and how they handle the service and whether they also despatch overseas, if this is appropriate to your needs.

With mail order, inserting literature into envelopes and arranging postage is a further back-up service that saves time and effort but is a cost that cannot be directly recovered, although it is probably worth it to one person businesses.

Production of sales literature is possibly the most important part of running this type of company and is a specialist art where it is again desirable to enlist the help of professional copywriters. It need not be expensive provided your instructions are explicit and the features and benefits of your product clearly identified. This is a one-off service, usually provided for a fee, but good copy is the key to obtaining sales.

Literature can be produced by computer and separate colours introduced for effect, but if your product contains photography it will pay to have it printed. This level of quality is probably outside the range of printing shops so you will need to find a good local printer. The cost in printing is in the origination and initial set up of machines which is spread across the number of leaflets wanted, i.e. 2,000 copies could be produced for not much more than 1,000, so if you plan to use the same leaflet several times it is far cheaper to have all batches printed immediately rather than on an as wanted basis.

The issue of where to send leaflets is also vitally important and lists can be rented from specialist brokers who have compiled lists of names under a variety of headings – lawyers, accountants, gardening enthusiasts, golf club members, etc. This enables you to define lists that are more likely to include prospective buyers of your product rather than a general mailing to the public at large. As you gain customers they become part of your specific list of names and should be held on a database.

You need to acquire a software package in order to build a database and be able to use it to issue printed envelopes or labels and to despatch emails simultaneously to everybody on the lists. You may need assistance from an IT specialist in order to accomplish this. Such people tend to charge on an hourly basis or could be brought in on a contract basis to handle each circular over the internet.

## Sales agents

Salesmen are often regarded as extroverts when in fact they are carrying out quite a lonely occupation. They spend time in cars and are very much on their own when putting across a pitch to customers and prospects. In the role they have chosen they have little need of help from other professionals or services other than ensuring they work out the best contractual terms at the front end, and possibly an accountant's services for dealing with annual accounts and tax returns. They do, of course, need ongoing support from their principals.

## Creative people

As stated in an earlier chapter, creative people are not really in business until they have created something unless creating for specific organisations under contractual arrangements. Once they have created a product, there is probably a need for a specialist agent. Actors and actresses are almost obliged to work through agents as indeed do musicians and composers. Authors, playwrights and poets are best advised to retain the services of a literary agent and artists usually need some form of support or sponsorship. Virtually all of these types of agents work on commission so are obviously motivated to obtain the best deal for you.

Inventors and designers are probably better advised to find a business agent rather than lawyers or accountants and may, in specific cases, need assistance from patent agents if they have something new. At the very least they should claim copyright on drawings and designs with the date of first publication shown. Contracts of this nature are highly variable and likely to depend on how much knowledge you have of probable buyers or users of the design or invention. There is likely to be an initial fee for research with a further commission on sales.

Once established you are likely to need to consult lawyers on contracts and retain accountants to deal with accounts and tax matters as advised to other single person businesses.

## Dealing with banks

This is being treated as a common subject to all readers as banks do not have different products for different trades and their contracts and terms vary only according to the view they take of risk and security available.

Hard to believe in modern times, when most banks are in a parlous state, but their business is all about lending money. They charge businesses for banking services but it is unlikely that such charges collectively cover their administrative costs. There is a major review of how banks operate and are regulated taking place currently, but this is unlikely to interfere with the services and lending arrangements they provide to the small business sector other than the shortage of funds is causing them to be more cautious in their lending policies.

In simple terms banks offer two types of facility – overdrafts and/or loans.

### Overdrafts

Essentially, an overdraft is a short-term facility with a limit as to how much you may be overdrawn. The facility is negotiated annually but the small print always advises that any money borrowed is repayable on demand. This clause is rarely exercised unless your business is in trouble but, when triggered, it means that all money that comes into your account is used to reduce the overdraft and any cheques you write will not be honoured and all standing orders and direct debits will not be met until the overdraft is repaid.

Unless the overdraft is secured, the bank is technically in the same position as any other creditor you deal with from a legal point of view so you could, in fact, open an account with another bank and pay money you receive into that account so that you are able to go on trading. There are further complications if your business goes under, at which point your personal assets are at risk, but that is an issue I will deal with later. The essential point is that the facility can be withdrawn at any time if the bank is concerned about the viability of your business.

In practice the banks normally charge an arrangement fee of around £100 up to a £5,000 limit, and up to £200 for anything higher. It is unlikely that most banks would lend above £10,000 to a sole trader without security unless you have a few years' track record of profitable trading. It is important to recognise that an overdraft has a limit that you may borrow up to from time to time, and banks become concerned if you are always overdrawn and close to that limit most of the time. They view this as hard core borrowing, implying that your business is under-capitalised, i.e. it is propped up by the bank rather than funds you have provided or profits retained in the business. In such circumstances you should expect a letter pointing this out and suggesting a meeting to discuss the matter.

Apart from arrangement fees, banks charge interest, typically around one per cent per month for small, profitable businesses. The two charges together equate to substantially more than 12 per cent per annum, depending on how frequently you are overdrawn.

The normal situation is that overdrafts are agreed annually but you cannot be certain that the bank will automatically agree to the same level and this has been the cause of some concern in recent times in the small business sector where the occasional squeeze has been applied.

### Loans

Quite frequently, banks will suggest that hard core borrowing is converted to a loan with monthly repayment terms agreed. Interest rates are usually higher than for overdrafts and front end loaded. This means that most of the interest is charged in the early months of the loan so that if you repay the full amount early you save very little interest. Terms vary, but usually loans are for three or five years and occasionally longer if used to purchase longer life assets. In the types of business we have been discussing there is unlikely to be a requirement for significant spending on assets. The largest item is likely to be a car or van where other options are available and probably cheaper. The most usual is lease purchase where a trade-in value is built into the financing package. This is a good arrangement for smaller businesses. It means you are effectively paying the depreciation monthly, plus an interest charge for the facility, but never actually own the vehicle. There are tax implications with vehicles which I will also discuss later.

### Security

While banks are willing to provide modest sums to small businesses and individuals their normal practice is to lend on security. This means pledging other realisable assets such as shares, or property. For most people who are starting a business with limited means and who need to raise additional funds to set themselves up, this usually means allowing the bank to take a second charge on your house. Second means that the original lender, usually a building society or another bank, has a prior right to repayment in the event of a sale and that the bank will have first claim on anything left over, ahead of other creditors. If there is a shortfall, the bank will rank equal to other creditors in respect of the shortfall. There are, however, special rules in the event of bankruptcy, dealt with later.

Under circumstances currently prevailing, the banks are trying to avoid selling houses where owners are in arrears with repayments. Government is applying pressure to avoid people being made homeless for political reasons. Banks are obliged to make provision for losses the moment they foreclose. The general experience is that enforced sales of houses are usually sold below comparable market prices. They will usually therefore explore all options before making you homeless but they can and do enforce the sale of homes in order to recover money owing to them.

In some cases where it is evident that you do have assets the bank may ask for a personal guarantee whereby you (or a friend or relative) undertake to settle the outstanding debt in the event of your business defaulting. A second option that is used where the business has been trading for some time and has assets in the business is to take a debenture over the assets, sometimes called a fixed and floating charge. The fixed element relates to permanent assets such as cars or equipment; the floating charge is over assets that are constantly changing, mainly debtors or money owed to the business. Clearly it would be messy if the bank claimed all the money paid to you by customers, but by using a floating charge they are saying the debtors that exist if and when they need to call in the loan. Again this means the bank will be able to sell the assets and collect the debts without reference to other creditors and ahead of them. They usually appoint receivers to do this, but such cases are extremely rare with one person businesses.

The whole concept of security is that the bank has a charge over asset(s) that it can realise and obtain payment therefore ahead of everybody else or, in the case of personal guarantees, seek immediate payment from the guarantor. However, such exercises only happen in the event of failure. This book is about how to succeed in business.

### How to raise bank finance

As with most things in life, you have to try and understand the other person's point of view. Banks need to lend money but do not want to lose it. It follows that they need to be reassured you are an honest person who runs a successful business or, if not yet started, that you are capable of doing so. They will usually ask you to provide a business plan or finance proposal, setting out your expectations and requirements, defining how the money will be used and how funds will flow through your business and, of course, how the money will be repaid.

Unless you have experience of preparing these plans you will need to sit down with your accountant and ask them to prepare it. In doing so do recognise that it needs major input from you. Your accountant cannot be expected to know your trade or much about the markets you operate in so prepare these sections yourself. The accountant's input will be more about cash flow statements and calculating how much you need and how quickly you are able to make repayment.

The plan should include around one page of typed A4 paper on each of the following:

- **Background** – Who are you? What experience do you have? Why are you going into business? How do you see the opportunities ahead of you?

- **The market and competition** – Who are you intending to serve or supply? What are the going rates and/ or prices and margins? Who are the established competitors and how do they operate? Have you found a niche you can specialise in supplying? How will the market develop over the next few years?

- **The marketing plan** – How will you promote yourself? What advantages do you have over existing competition? How will you exploit them? What contacts do you have? How will you price the product/service? What resources do you need to carry out the plan?

- **Trading projections** – Sales forecasts for three years, less expenses to show net margins and net profits.

- **Capital expenditure requirements** – What are you planning to buy, i.e. computers, printers, database, furniture and fitments, car, etc? What do they cost? How much are you contributing?

- **Cash flow projections** – These should set out the timing of expenditure month by month and progression of monthly sales reflecting the difference between income and expenditure month by month. Ideally this should show peak borrowings during the first six months that is gradually reduced as income grows until repayment is made.

- **Summary (at the front)** – Two sentences on background and then state how much money is needed and what for, followed by a short paragraph on the market and how it will be exploited due to particular advantages. The next paragraph should highlight, in tabular form, sales less expense to show net profits for each of the three years ahead. State, in the final paragraph, the peak funding requirement and the length of time needed to repay, and ask for the money.

The whole needs only to run to five or six pages, plus three pages of cash flow projections, and should be neatly typed and presented in a folder, with an extra copy for the bank manager in case he has to refer it. Generally I prefer to present these documents rather than send them through the post. Business is actually done between people and it as well to present yourself and talk about your business with a measure of enthusiasm, guide the manager through the sections and answer his questions. If you are dealing with the bank at sufficiently senior level you will probably receive an immediate decision, if not, it may take a few days.

# 12 *A basic understanding of commercial law*

The next four chapters deal with practical and legal aspects of being in business and how the law affects you. The moment you start a business you are immediately subject to a plethora of rules and regulations. Most businessmen argue too many, and political parties of all persuasions argue in favour of cutting red tape, but never quite seem to get round to doing so. At present, however, you are immediately subject to registering as self-employed and setting up a direct debit so that a monthly National Insurance charge can be extracted from your bank account. Registration, of course, notifies the Inland Revenue that you have set up a business that will be subject to tax. The first instalment is due by 31 January, following the end of your first year of trading. You gain a short break, but should set aside funds to meet the future liability. Tax implications and structuring are dealt with in the next chapter, but to register simply go to the HMRC website, follow the instructions and complete the form required and take a copy.

As soon as you employ anybody (see Chapter 14), you are subject to further rules and regulations and must set up a payroll to deduct taxes and National Insurance from employees' remuneration. There are rules about health and safety at work and, of course, health and safety regulations surrounding the work you carry out for customers. These are insurable risks. You need to take out cover for damage to third parties and or damage caused by your product or service.

Most people are familiar with how insurance works, certainly everyone who owns a car and most householders, but in carrying out your everyday work you may cause damage to other people or their property. It is easy to envisage dropping something from a ladder or scaffold that lands on somebody's head, or maims them. You might work on the foundations of a semi-detached house or party wall and, in doing so, damage the property next door. Insurance cover is obligatory for this type of risk, so do consult an insurance broker early and talk through the cover you need. I will deal separately with life cover and pensions later.

Professionals can also cause damage negligently. An architect could design a building that has a flawed construction and is ultimately unsafe. A lawyer could misinterpret the law applying to a particular subject and put a client to considerable expense or assign the wrong plot of land in a property sale. Auditors could neglect to examine ownership documents and subsequently be held liable for not reporting to shareholders that the assets no longer existed. These failings too can be covered by professional indemnity insurance.

Commerce operates within a framework of law. Most of the time this is implicitly understood by the parties but occasionally spills over into an argument. It is as well, therefore, to understand the basic principles of the law. This is not so that you avoid using lawyers, merely a guide to comprehend the legal implications of what you are doing in broad terms.

## Contract law

This impinges on every transaction. Contracts do not have to be in writing unless relating to the transfer of real estate or shares. To be valid a contract needs only three constituents:

**Offer – acceptance – and consideration**

In simple terms if you say to your friend: 'I will take you to the cinema tonight if you do the washing up', and if the friend says yes, or does the washing up, you have a binding contract that stands up in law.

Similarly if somebody says: 'How much to fix my boiler?'

You reply: 'Hundred quid.'

The customer says: 'Okay.'

There is a binding contract. It may not have covered all aspects of what is involved, i.e. there is no commitment to repair the boiler today but, nevertheless, there is an obligation on both parties. In such cases it would be implicit that the work be carried out within a reasonable time, but there is a potential argument about how much is reasonable.

There can be counter offers and extended negotiations, but the contract will only exist if the above three constituents are present. It is also self evident that if you have spent considerable time negotiating the conditions surrounding the offer, consideration and acceptance you would be wise to put them in writing. However valid, there is an obvious problem with a verbal contract in that, unless witnessed, it is open to dispute as to who said what, i.e. 'You told me you would fix it on Tuesday.' 'No I didn't. I said Tuesday week.'

It follows there is less doubt about the terms agreed if the contract is in writing or can be evidenced by written documents. A letter confirming the agreement following a meeting would have more credibility than somebody arguing that he or she had not agreed with the letter. You can quickly see that it pays to be disciplined and to confirm the arrangement in writing. This can be done briefly or you can use order acknowledgements in printed form that thank the customer for the order, confirms when and how much.

This can be further improved by having your terms and conditions printed on the reverse of the order acknowledgement. If you cannot set these out simply yourself invite a solicitor to draft them for you but try to present them in user friendly terms not 'small print' with all its implications.

Before leaving this subject there is a further point that can be critical relating to variations. This frequently happens when a customer has a tradesman on site and says: 'I wonder if you could just fix that for me while you're here.'

The tradesman agrees and finds it takes them an extra day and submits a bill, but they have a problem. The additional work was carried out without 'consideration'. There was merely offer and acceptance unless in their order acknowledgement the tradesman had stated that any additional work carried out on site would be charged at so much extra.

It is easy to slip up on small variations and this even happens with large institutions that put everything in writing. For instance, somebody is paying off a large debt to a credit card company at £50 a month and makes an offer to pay £3,000 in full and final settlement of a £10,000 debt. The credit card company writes back and says: 'We reject your offer of £3,000 and suggest £7,000 or continue paying £50 per month until the debt is extinguished.' The creditor continues paying £50 per month, seemingly ignoring the correspondence but, in fact, a new contract has been created. The credit card company has discarded its former contractual right to demand income and expenditure statements and to vary the level of repayment. Inadvertently it made a new contract and must continue accepting £50 per month for the next 17 years. Your printed terms and conditions should cover this type of risk.

## Sale of goods

It is implicit that goods must be fit for purpose, regardless of whether they are guaranteed or not or subject to warranties. If something is purchased for the advertised or described purpose and does not fulfil that requirement it can be returned and must be replaced or refunded.

Similarly if you provide samples, prior to sale, and the bulk of the consignment does not match the samples, the whole consignment can be rejected. In practice this tends to lead to negotiations rather than litigation. You can agree to sort the consignment and take back the inferior products or agree a discount.

**Agency** also needs understanding in that, in general terms, somebody acting as your agent can commit you and acts with your full authority as regards third parties. In practice terms of reference should be clarified in writing with your agent, making clear the situations in which they should refer back to you for guidance when acting on your behalf. If you do not like the agreement reached in your name you should quickly write to the customer or supplier pointing out that your agent has exceeded their authority and offer to renegotiate, but if they hold you to the contract your only action is against your agent. Again, in practical terms, you will start by withholding their commission and any money owing to them, repudiate their contract and have sufficient sanctions to ensure that they don't stray outside of their brief.

In circumstances such as this the contract should be in writing, but more of this when I deal with employment although it should be noted that an agent is not an employee.

# 13 *Tax implications and structuring*

Many years ago a self-employed person could delay paying tax for up to three years when starting out, which helped to nurse capital and give some headroom to get the business off the ground, but not so in modern times. You must immediately register the fact you are in business with the Department of Work and Pensions (DWP) who will set up a direct debit to charge £2.70 per week to your account in respect of Class 2 contributions. A further levy is made annually on profits. You also register with HM Revenue and Customs through the Helpline for the Newly Self-Employed. They allocate a tax reference number, send a short questionnaire, followed by a tax return for you to complete and file.

The Income Tax year runs from 6 April to the following 5 April. In practice the Revenue accept the year to 31 March as meaning the same thing. It should be noted, however, that the business year does not have to coincide with the tax year. If you start a business in July you may decide to produce your first accounts to the following 31 July. The Revenue will apportion profits from start up to the following 5 April.

The tax rates and allowances are the same for all individuals other than pensioners who receive a higher personal (tax free) allowance, subject to not having other sources of income. This advantage will be withdrawn in the near future as pensions are increased across the board. The personal allowance is currently set at £9,440 but with a government pledge to increase it during this Parliament to £10,000. The standard rate of 20 per cent is charged on the next £32,010 earned, thereafter the rate increases to 40 per cent. National Insurance, in effect another income tax, kicks in at £7,755 per year and thereafter at 9 per cent on the next £33,695. There is a further 2 per cent NI surcharge on profits above £42,475, and income above this figure is taxed at 40 per cent. Those with incomes above £100,000 p.a. lose their personal allowance and a 50 per cent tax rate kicks in above £150,000 income p.a. Most of these rates and allowances are subject to change with each budget, but the framework is likely to remain for the next several years.

Employees have these taxes deducted from salaries and wages under PAYE and indeed suffer higher rates of National Insurance. The self-employed, however, are unable to claim unemployment benefit when out of work. The self-employed are obliged to write cheques twice yearly to cover these obligations. They pay half the tax and National Insurance based on the previous

year's income in advance of the tax year ending on 5
April by 31 January each year and a second instalment
by 31 July. Adjustment is made the following January if
profits for the actual year vary from the previous year.

These rates imply a levy of almost 21 per cent at the
average income of £25,000 p.a. This climbs to 26
per cent at twice the average wage, say £50,000. At
£500,000 p.a. the rate has climbed to over 46 per cent.
This is a substantial income, of course, but suddenly
seems considerably less when the Government has
creamed off £230,000. It is unsurprising that people
look for ways to avoid this swingeing impost on their
creativity and effort. The majority of readers of this
book, however, are probably more concerned with
generating incomes above £50,000, possibly pushing to
modestly in excess of £100,000 where tax and National
Insurance will take up 25–30 per cent of their incomes.
So what can you do about it?

## Record keeping

The first and most obvious thing is to ensure that you
fully record every expense that can be set against your
income – postage, stationery, telephone, travel, etc. The
rule here is that all such expenditure must be 'wholly
and exclusively' for the purposes of the business. This is
very tough wording and, in reality, there are many grey
areas, i.e. you might use a bedroom in your house as an
office. It obviously saves a rental and makes commercial
sense but the Revenue could argue it isn't exclusively
for business. In practice a compromise is usually agreed.

If you dedicate one room in your house exclusively for business use in say a six-room house, exclusive of kitchen and bathrooms, you could claim one-sixth of your rent, community charges, heating and lighting, etc. A word of caution here, however, that by doing so some councils might apply a business rate as well as council tax and part of your house could be deemed a business asset for Capital Gains Tax. You could also agree the costs of fitting the room out with desk, computer, filing cabinets, etc. as assets purchased for the business. Expenditure of this nature cannot be offset against income as it is deemed to have a life and so allowances can be charged annually against the income, effectively writing the assets off over a number of years.

The Revenue will usually agree a percentage of the cost of a car as private usage, say 20 per cent and allow you to charge 80 per cent of the running cost against your income, but there are further restrictions on capital cost so it often pays to own the car outside of the business and invoice the business with mileage charges for business trips. You can also charge technical journals, even newspapers and beverages against income.

The implications of all this, of course, are that you must obtain receipts and keep records of expenses but, clearly, once you are in a position to save 40 per cent of the cost of all such expenses it pays to be disciplined.

You can also employ your spouse or partner, although this is of marginal advantage if they are already in employment unless you are definitely a higher rate taxpayer. Keeping the records is, of course, a job you can allocate together with taking messages when you are out, doing the filing, paying invoices and chasing up payment of your outstanding invoices. You could deem this to be a job at £7,500 p.a. paid to your spouse, free of tax and National Insurance, but chargeable against your income. You can arrive at a position that is acceptable to the Revenue, roughly as follows:

| | | |
|---|---|---|
| Income say | | 60,000 |
| Materials purchased | 4,000 | |
| Salary to spouse | 7,500 | |
| Share of rent, etc. | 2,000 | |
| Mileage charge 12,000 miles | 4,500 | |
| Travel | 1,500 | |
| Incidentals | 500 | |
| | | 20,000 |
| Taxable income | | 40,000 |

There are of course a multitude of rules and regulations covering every aspect of this type of calculation but we are concerned here only with principles, and most small businesses find it worthwhile to employ an accountant to produce these figures and advise on what can and cannot be done. This usually costs less than £1,000 per annum but, as seen above, failure to keep records and take advantage of available relief could cost you nearly £7,000 p.a. in the above example.

## Operating through a limited company

There is a loophole for higher tax payers who can run their business through a limited company. Business owner and spouse could each take a salary of £7,500 tax free and could agree to split the share capital say 75 per cent: 25 per cent, reflecting their relative contributions to the business. Thereafter they each take monthly or quarterly dividends.

Salaries are allowed as an expense against income but dividends are not, but deemed to be paid out of the company's after tax income and further deemed to have suffered tax in the hands of the recipient and so are net of tax, provided their income, plus deemed tax of 10 per cent, does not exceed £41,450 currently. In this manner they have avoided the National Insurance levy of 9 per cent on £33,695 or £3,033 per annum, plus 2 per cent surcharge above £41,450. The accountancy cost of doing this might be as much as £1,000 p.a. higher, but usually less. Most one person businesses operating at this level would save a minimum of £3,000 p.a. in National Insurance contributions alone and probable further tax savings so it is worth considering once you are reasonably sure your income will always exceed £50,000 p.a.

Again there are legal implications in owning a company. The first and most important point to note is that a company has its own identity. It is not an extension of you. It is owned by the shareholders who usually, but not necessarily, have equal voting rights and is operated by the directors who do not have to be shareholders although obviously would be in the circumstances we are discussing. Company Law is again another large subject but for most small companies you must file accounts in statutory form within ten months of your year end at Companies House and file a Corporation Tax Return.

There are many other taxes, including Capital Gains, Corporation and Inheritance taxes, most of which should not come into focus until you have a well-established business and have accumulated additional resources.

## Value added tax (VAT)

This is an important source of revenue for government but should, in practice, be neutral on businesses in so far as they charge an additional tax to their customers and claim back any VAT they have paid to suppliers. The ultimate charge is, of course, borne by the general public who cannot register or claim back any VAT they pay. It can be argued, of course, that VAT does have an impact on business in that it makes the ultimate price of products purchased by the public more expensive and this may stifle sales.

Certain products like food, books, newspapers, financial services and clothing are exempt but all other businesses must register for VAT immediately they achieve sales or fees of £77,000 currently. This is done by completing a VAT application form and submitting it to the VAT Registration Unit in Wolverhampton who ultimately issue you with a VAT number which must appear on all your invoices and you must account, usually quarterly, for all VAT charged and any deductions you make must be supported by VAT invoices issued to you. The current rate is 20 per cent with effect from January 2011.

Sales and services provided outside of Europe are VAT exempt, hence an exporter may claim back any VAT paid to suppliers. Sales and services provided to customers within Europe are also exempt provided your customer is registered for VAT in that country. If not, VAT must be charged. If selling extensively to non-registered customers, like the general public, in EEC countries you may find it necessary to register in that country once sales achieve the registration threshold. In such cases you will need professional guidance in that country.

# 14 *Employing staff*

It is inevitable that as your business grows you will
need help to get things done but, as stated in an earlier
chapter, you should sub-contract to outside businesses
for as long as possible. The point here is that you
have a known expense for an agreed service and can
build it into your prices with only a limited risk it will
overshoot. The second advantage is that an outside
person in business will usually know what he is doing
and has an interest in being efficient. Unfortunately
this is not true of a significant proportion of employees.
Their primary objective is a steady income and, unless
you can build in a practical incentive, they are not
motivated to do other than what is basically expected
of them. I know these are hard words that will offend
many people who are dedicated to their jobs but, even
they will recognise a certain truth in what I say.

A further important point is that their cost to you is
significantly more than the salary you pay. You have to
pay Employer's National Insurance, now running at 13.8

per cent of salary and a tempting target for governments who are short of money. Holiday entitlements and public holidays are such that you are lucky if you get 45 five-day weeks per annum out of them and they require space and facilities to work. This could be difficult if you are still running the business from home. More importantly they have to be managed, guided and trained and this is likely to take up a proportion of your own time, making you less efficient at generating the income you need to pay them and keep the business viable. It is sad but true that as many small businesses expand in sales and employees their profits do not keep pace. Nevertheless, the time will come when you need ongoing day-to-day help to manage your business but it is vital to approach this in a logical and professional manner and to confront certain truths about yourself.

## Your own role in the business

Define your own strengths and weaknesses. What do you like doing most? What don't you like doing? Are you a people person or do you prefer dealing with the technical aspects of the job? Are you a good communicator and teacher? Are you a leader or a bit of a bully?

These are important questions because what you are about to embark on is building a team, progressively, to make your business more successful and, particularly in a small business, people have to like and respect other team members. Mutual inter-dependence and trust are more important than individual brilliance.

## The job description

Having considered your own role and strengths honestly it is probable that you will want to concentrate on those and this clearly leaves a gap. It may be that you are a poor administrator and that what you really need is somebody to take the paperwork off your hands. If so, you then need to set out precisely what is involved. Is it merely someone to keep the records or do you want somebody to range more widely and prepare estimates and quotations or do you want somebody to organise selling activities? Perhaps you are a good all-rounder who pays close attention and what you really want is a general assistant, a man or girl Friday.

Be very clear about what you do want and keep a touch of realism. If you do want somebody to organise selling and promoting the business, don't expect them to fill their spare time by doing the bookkeeping too. Finally, having thought about how the intended appointee integrates with you, write the job description in simple terms.

As an example let us assume you are a former HR manager in a significant business and you have built up a business by supplying bespoke employees' handbooks that set out disciplinary procedures, sickness rules, holiday entitlements, etc. to small- and medium-sized companies. Your main strengths are that you are good in front of the customer and at getting the business and analysing the client's situation but, you hate cold calling and making appointments and you become bored with writing the reports. Nevertheless, you believe that if you could obtain more client meetings you could win much more business and you could handle it efficiently if you didn't have to write so many reports.

Now we can start to write the job specification.

1. Make telesales calls to set up meetings for proprietor.

2. Design leaflets to be sent to all prospects who agree to a meeting.

3. Create a standard framework to be used as employees' handbooks.

4. Design a standard questionnaire for all clients that can be used to adapt standard handbook into a bespoke handbook.

5. Produce bespoke handbooks for agreement with proprietor and client.

## Job advertisement

If you have prepared the job description thoroughly, the advert almost writes itself, but you need to consider what kind of person would fit the role.

Do they need a background in HR? Probably not, but they must be good communicators on the telephone and in writing. Some creativity and initiative is desirable and they must be a self-starter and be capable of working on their own without supervision.

Is age critical? Probably not, but you want somebody flexible who can grow with the business and, of course, they must have some experience so you could set a lower age limit of 25, although with age discrimination it might be wiser to say that anybody under the age of 25 is unlikely to have sufficient experience. Your own preferences also come into the reckoning. Do you want to work with somebody significantly older than yourself? If not, this limits the upper age limit to say 45 although you may not declare this.

Is fitness important? Could a disabled person do the job and, of course, you cannot discriminate by race or sex.

Finally, how much are you willing to pay, bearing in mind that the cost to you is more than the advertised salary? The answer to this can be measured by the effect on the business. Let us assume you are generating a fee income of circa £120,000 and incur £20,000 of current business expenses, but by off-loading the described function you could increase fee income by up to a further £100,000 p.a. You could reasonably pay a third of this to your administrator who will, of course, attract further business expenses. They will need space to work in, a desk, chair, filing cabinet and spend time on the telephone, use stationery, post letters, etc. The overall effect is that the extra £100,000 in fees could result in a further £50,000 profit. If it doesn't, why do it?

Almost certainly you will advertise locally in the press or notify the job centre or, if you are pressed for time, you could use a recruitment agency. Their fees vary between 15 and 25 per cent of first year salary. However handled, it is better to seek written applications, complete with CV, as this quickly shows the type of experience candidates have gained and whether they are job hoppers, and the manner in which their careers have developed. Have they spent a few years in each job? Did they change jobs to take on more responsibility? This helps you gain an overall impression and, if you have received a good response, a basis for selecting a few candidates for interview.

---

### WANTED

A Sales Administrator to assist busy proprietor engaged in HR consultancy. This role involves setting up meetings, producing company literature and mailing to prospects and assisting with creating a framework to standardise product services for tailoring to client needs.

The ideal candidate will have a background in sales administration and/or marketing and be a good communicator. Salary negotiable in the range £25–£30,000.

Apply in writing to:

---

## The job interview

The first thing to say is that it helps if you like your new employee but do not select purely on that basis. Put the candidates at ease and recognise that being interviewed

for a job may be a stressful situation for them so start
with a few soft questions about their families and wider
interests. Thereafter try to let them talk about what
they do in their current job and mentally measure
how it fits with your requirements. Ask about their
earlier experience and what they have achieved in each
occupation. Ask how they perceive their own strengths
and weaknesses. Make notes, even take a photograph if
mutually acceptable, then allow them to question you
about your own background and the business you have
created. Bear in mind they may have other employment
opportunities.

It is reasonable and probably expected that you want to
mull over how the applicant fits with your needs and
against other candidates but some feedback is desirable.
For example:

'I still have three further interviews to conduct but
you do fit my specification reasonably well. Are you
up for any other jobs?' If 'Yes': 'Please give me a call
before you accept any alternative offer. I should be in a
position to reach a decision by Friday.'

Alternatively you might say: 'Thanks for coming to
see me but I really don't think you match what I am
looking for so I would rather tell you direct than leave
you hanging on waiting for a letter. Good luck with
your future career.'

If you cannot make your mind up between two prospects then call them back for a second meeting and explain your indecision. A further meeting will usually help clarify your thoughts.

## Contract of employment

The appointment letter should be in the nature of a contract:

Dear . . .

Further to our recent discussions I am pleased to confirm my offer to appoint you as sales administrator in my business at a salary of £25,000 p.a., paid monthly. This is subject to a trial period of three months and thereafter will become a permanent position subject to one month's notice of termination by either party.

The main functions of your role are set out in the attached job specification but you may from time to time be required to assist me with other aspects of running the business. Your performance will be reviewed annually and if good progress is made your salary will be adjusted upwards.

Paid holidays will be accrued at one and a quarter days for each month of service to an ultimate level of three weeks per annum in addition to the normal public holidays.

If these terms are satisfactory please sign the duplicate copy of this letter and send it to me. I also take the opportunity to welcome you into the business and trust we will have a long and mutually satisfactory association.

Yours sincerely

## Affirmation of the contract

By returning the duplicate letter your appointee has entered into a contract with you as defined in the letter. Also, by insisting on holidays being accrued you avoid the risk of your new employee leaving after six months and demanding a full annual holiday entitlement.

Strictly speaking you should have a disciplinary procedure but in a one man business it is not essential to set this out. If your employee isn't up to scratch, however, you must set out their shortcomings in a formal warning and allow time for them to show improvement before dismissal. Under present law you cannot arbitrarily fire employees other than for serious breaches of contract or felony. You can of course remove them during the trial period or immediately after.

# 15 Acquiring or renting property

Think long and hard before entering into a property contract and, unless you have adequate funds, do not consider purchasing commercial property. It is a specialist area and also a myth that property prices always increase. They do not and are usually at their lowest when there is a shortage of money and the business situation is tough. Yes, people do make money out of property but it can be a distraction from your main business and you must be clear about your main objective. Once established your business pays for everything so you cannot normally allow the business to slide.

If, however, you have good reasons for not working from home you should first consider how much space you really need rather than what you would like. Rentals are usually calculated per square foot. Next consider location and style. Will clients visit you? If not, you might be able to find a small office on an industrial estate where rents are lower and you have adequate parking. If, on the other hand, property is part of your business image or you are in the retail business you probably have to work in or close to a town centre and will have to consider additional factors, like access or customer parking, reception areas, etc.

There are essentially three types of renting arrangements, the most common of which is:

## A lease

This is usually a term contract with many pitfalls for the unwary. The landlord is likely to have other properties so is in the business as a professional who employs a solicitor to draw up a standard agreement, the standard being from the landlord's point of view. Typically, this is going to require you to pay in advance, usually quarterly with no right of offset against any shortcomings by the landlord. It will also commit you to paying for the full term, i.e. even if you fall ill and cannot continue in business you will have to continue paying the rent for the full term of the agreement. It is, however normal to have a break clause, say after three years in a six-year agreement and you may have the right to sublet part or all of the area you rent. As an absolute minimum you should ensure such clauses are included in your lease.

It is likely that any property you rent is part of a larger property with other tenants who are obliged to share common facilities such as toilets, kitchens, staircases, etc., all of which have to be maintained. The entire building will have to be redecorated from time to time so, as one of the beneficiaries, you will be required to meet your share of these costs, usually as an additional service charge.

For reasons I have never understood leases seem to need 50 to 100 pages of typescript to incorporate all the parties' obligations and usually have a termination clause that requires you to hand back the property in good condition. This too is a trap for the unwary. It could be that you moved into the property when it was in poor condition with worn-out carpets and possibly dry rot. You could, nevertheless, find yourself responsible for treating the dry rot and replacing the carpets on termination. This is extreme but most leases have a requirement to redecorate internally at the end of the term and to rectify dilapidations. This too is weighted against the tenant because the lease is sure to include a clause that in the event of dispute an independent surveyor will be appointed at the tenant's expense.

Seen from the landlord's viewpoint these conditions are not unreasonable as tenants have been known to cause considerable damage to property they rent. The point, however, is that you face costs significantly higher than the quoted rent when signing a lease and, of course, you have to pay the rates on the property. Small businesses can usually recoup some of the rates so it is worth enquiring about this from the local Council before signing.

## Sub-tenancies

As stated above, most tenants secure a right to sublet part or all the property they lease. In some cases they may have signed a lease that provides more space than actually needed but which possibly secures a desired location. A shop with offices above might fall into this category although most landlords would probably divide such a property into two leases. Quite often, however, some tenants find themselves with excess space which they would like to sublet to obtain a contribution to the overall cost of the premises. Their lease probably requires approval from the landlord to sublet and may require them to apply the full terms of the lease. This can be unrealistic, however, when they are part way through the term and merely looking to mitigate their expenses. Such circumstances provide opportunities to negotiate.

You should expect to pay the going rent, inclusive of rates or community charges and service charge, but should seek to avoid any terminal payments as an absolute minimum. You may be able to negotiate the going rate downwards depending on the tenant's circumstances and the desirability and demand for such amounts of space in your locality. You should, in any case, ask to see the head lease and ask your solicitor to cast an eye over it and point out any potentially onerous clauses that you would try to ensure are not passed on to you in any agreement you sign.

You do not have to comply with the terms of the head lease or even sign up for the full term. You cannot, however, extend the term beyond the end of the head lease without entering into a new contract, but you may have adequate accommodation available for a known term; sufficient to establish your business and be able to look again at future requirements towards the end of the period without cost penalties on termination.

## Licences

This concept is growing in popularity because it meets the needs of small, one person businesses. Several property companies have acquired buildings that they convert into a number of offices within, that will accommodate from one to six people and the owners provide a range of back-up services. These can include meeting rooms on an as needed basis, provision of a telephone answering service, telephones, a communal photocopying facility, reception service, office cleaning, etc. In other cases it can be as simple as just the rent of one unit.

The advantages of this arrangement are that you pay for additional facilities on an as needed basis and that you sign up for a short period, say six months and, thereafter, can quit at one month's notice. This flexibility is desirable, particularly for new start-ups.

## Other

Not everybody wants an office or shop. It may be you have a need for storage space or a workshop that might be satisfied with a simple lock-up garage or small warehouse or a unit on an industrial estate.

These arrangements are usually negotiable short-term contracts and, in most parts of the UK, are readily available.

# 16 *Expansion problems*

A surprisingly large number of businesses ultimately fail after becoming established and starting to expand. The underlying reason is usually because they expand beyond the capacity of the owner to manage in detail and grow out of control.

The initial start up of a business is precarious and this is the reason I dealt with most of the issues on start up in the early chapters of this book. The risks, however, are relatively small when starting up if you have no serious investment at stake. As you start to expand into what I call the second stage risk, you have probably committed a few years of your life and accumulated resources that are deployed in the business. The downside has grown considerably.

We touched on this briefly in Chapter 14 on employment. As I stated then, you must ensure your business profits from employing people otherwise you are expanding merely for the sake of growing bigger and without the margin to deal with any reversal. It is often said in business that if you are not going forward you are going backwards. There is a modicum of truth in this adage and a risk that, by turning business down, you can spread a negative message, but expansion should be treated with care.

It is self-evident, however, that you can reach the limit of your capacity in the trades and professions where your prices are related to time. You must eventually run out of time and there is a limit to how many hours you can devote to business if you want to retain any semblance of a private life. Nevertheless, if you are able to expand successfully you can develop your underlying wealth and look to a prosperous retirement.

## Know yourself

I began this book by saying that almost anybody of average intelligence can use their skills to develop a small one person business whatever their background or personality. I have elsewhere counselled from time to time that you should know yourself and understand your limitations. If your business relies on your skills you risk dissipating them by employing additional people to replicate them. You are now in a position of managing rather than working and this requires a different set of abilities. You have to be able to organise, delegate, lead and teach. Be absolutely honest with yourself. If this is not how you want to spend your life, don't do it. You will be much happier by increasing your prices and sticking to your core skills.

If you do want to grow, however, you must revert to first principles as outlined in the early chapters and redefine the opportunity but, with more now at stake than when you first set out, you must try to quantify it more precisely.

I include this brief chapter, however, because in business one is always thinking ahead, anticipating developments and planning the next stage. It is part of the reason why running your own business is so engrossing.

# Index

accountant, 120, 136
actors, 53
advertising, 61
  *see also* marketing
Adwords, 26
affiliate marketing, 25
agency
  and commercial law, 144
  market knowledge, 38
  setting up an, 26-8
artists, 29, 80-2, 102
*Artists' and Writers'*
  *Yearbook*, 78
aspirations, understanding
  your, 10-13
authors, 28-9, 78-80, 101

banks, 130-8
  loans, 133
  overdrafts, 131
  raising bank finance,
  135-8
  security, 133-5
believing in yourself, 12-13,
  40-1
business plan, 135-7
buying decision, 29-32

calculating risk and
  breakeven, 105-18

agents, 117
creative occupations,
  117-18
internet trading, mail
  order, etc., 113-16
management services to
  industry, 112-13
personal services, 109
professional services,
  110-12
trade services to the
  public, 107-9
Capital Gains Tax, 149
catchment area, 14
charging for your services,
  7-8
  *see also* pricing
Clique Bank, 26
cold calling, 67
commercial law, 139-45
  agency, 144
  contract law, 141-4
  sale of goods, 144-5
communication, 11
competition, 33-9, 41
  services to industry, 36
  services to the public,
  33-6
competitors, 35
concept, 56

creativity, 28, 52

database, 23, 66, 75
Department of Work and
    Pensions (DWP), 146
designers, 29, 56, 103
differentiate, 34, 41, 50, 60
Dunn & Bradstreet, 21, 23

eBay, 37
Employer's National
    Insurance, 154
employing staff, 154-62
  affirmation of the
    contract, 162
  contract of employment,
    161-2
  job advertisement, 1579
  job description, 156-7
  job interview, 159-61
  your own role, 155
expansion problems, 169-71

financial markets, 25
freelance writing, 53

goals, setting realistic, 12
Google, 26
Google Local, 60

Helpline for the Newly Self-
    Employed, 146
HM Revenue and Customs,
    146

information publishing, 25
Inland Revenue, 120
insurances, 121, 140
internet, 14, 18, 25, 37
inventors, 29, 54-5, 56,
    82-5, 103
investment, 1, 5

Jordans, 21, 23

*Key British Enterprises*, 21

limitations, 57, 170

mail-shot, 67
market analysis, 20, 41
market, defining your, 14-32
  management services,
    20-3
  personal services, 17-18
  professional services,
    18-20
  skilled trades, 14-16
  trading, mail order and
    internet, 24
marketing, 59-85
  creative people, 77-82
  dealing with the
    competition, 62-3
  general trading, internet
    and mail order, 75-7
  inventors, 82-5
  personal services, 63-5
  professional services, 65-6

sales agents, 71-4
selling the benefits, 61-2,
   64, 66, 70
services to industry, 66-71
skilled trades, 59-63
medical professions, 6
meetings, 69
muli-level marketing, 26
musicians, 53

National Insurance, 147
niche, 50
numbers, 13

objectives, setting, 42
objectivity, 32

paperwork, 13.
party plan schemes, 26
people, 10-11
personal services, 5, 45-6
   *see also* calculating
      risk and breakeven;
      marketing; pricing;
      service-based business;
      using other services and
      professionals
photographers, 103
positive thinking, 12
presentation, 16
pricing, 34, 86-104
   agents, 100-1
   creative people, 101-4
   general trading, internet

and mail order, 97-100
   management services,
      94-7
   personal services, 91-2
   professional services, 92-4
   skilled trades, 87-91
product-based business, 4
professional services, 46
   *see also* calculating
      risk and breakeven;
      marketing; pricing;
      service-based business;
      using other services and
      professionals
property, acquiring or
      renting, 163-8
   a lease, 164-5
   licences, 167
   other, 167-8
   sub-tenancies, 166-7
public, dealing with, 10-11
pyramid selling, 27

records, keeping, 61, 148
reputation, 10, 12, 19
resumé, 16
risk, 6
   *see also* calculating risk
      and breakeven

self-employment
   advantages, 5-9
   benefits, 9
self-publishing, 53

selling the product or
    service, 11, 36
service-based business
    management services, 3
    personal services, 3
    professional services, 3
    starting, 1-4
services to commercial
    undertakings, 47-50
Shaw, Percy, 56
shelf-life, 58
skilled trades, 14-16, 43-5
    disputes, 89-90
    insurances, 91
    pricing, 87-8
    terms of trade, 89
Small Claims Court, 90
'so what' test, 50
specialisation, 46-7
staff costs, 119, 140
    *see also* employing staff
sub-contracting, 16

tax, 120, 139, 146-53
    operating through a
        limited company, 151-2
    record keeping, 148-51
    value added tax (VAT)
        152-3

terms of trade, 89, 92
test marketing, 28
Thompson Directories, 15
time, 35

using other services and
    professionals, 119-38
    creative people, 129-30
    dealing with banks, 130-8
    management services,
        126-7
    personal services, 124-5
    professional services, 126
    sales agents, 129
    selling via the internet,
        mail order, etc., 127-9
    tradesmen, 121-4

VAT (value added tax), 120,
    152-3

websites, 35, 66, 76
word of mouth, 12

*Yellow Pages*, 15, 17, 18, 33,
    42, 59